# I Have the Data...
# Now What?

## Analyzing Data and
## Making Instructional Changes

Betsy Moore

EYE ON EDUCATION
6 DEPOT WAYWEST, SUITE 106
LARCHMONT, NY 10538
(914) 833–0551
(914) 833–0761 fax
www.eyeoneducation.com

A sincere effort has been made to supply the identity of those who have created specific strategies. Any omissions have been unintentional.

**Library of Congress Cataloging-in-Publication Data**

Moore, Betsy.
  I have the data-- now what? : analyzing data and making instructional changes
/ by Betsy Moore.
    p. cm.
  ISBN 978-1-59667-170-6
  1.  Curriculum change--Statistical methods. 2.  Teaching--Statistical methods.
3.  Educational statistics.  I. Title.
  LB1570.M63 2010
  371.39--dc22

                                                                    2010036714

10 9 8 7 6 5 4 3 2 1

Production services provided by
Rick Soldin a Book/Print Production Specialist
www.book-comp.com

## Also Available from Eye On Education

**Formative Assessments in a Professional Learning Community**
Todd Stanley and Betsy Moore

**Critical Thinking and Formative Assessments:
Increasing the Rigor in Your Classroom**
Betsy Moore and Todd Stanley

**Short Cycle Assessment:
Improving Student Achievement through Formative Assessment**
Susan Lang, Todd Stanley, and Betsy Moore

**Response to Intervention and Continuous School Improvement:
Using Data, Vision, and Leadership to Design, Implement, and
Evaluate a Schoolwide Prevention System**
Victoria L. Bernhardt and Connie L. Hebert

**Data, Data Everywhere:
Bringing All the Data Together for Continuous School Improvement**
Victoria L. Bernhardt

**Data Analysis for Continuous School Improvement, 2nd Edition**
Victoria L. Bernhardt

**From Questions to Actions:
Using Questionnaire Data for Continuous School Improvement**
Victoria L. Bernhardt and Bradley Geise

**School Portfolio, 2nd Edition:
A Comprehensive Framework For School Improvement**
Victoria L. Bernhardt

**Data-Driven Decision Making and Dynamic Planning:
A School Leader's Guide**
Paul Preuss

**Data-Driven Instructional Leadership**
Rebecca Blink

**School Leader's Guide to Root Cause Analysis:
Using Data to Dissolve Problems**
Paul Preuss

This book is dedicated to my mother, Janet Wilkins Chappell, my mentor, my role model, and my inspiration. Thank you for giving me the confidence to follow in your footsteps and for showing me what a true "Master Teacher" is.

# Meet the Author

Betsy Moore is a veteran teacher who retired from Reynoldsburg City Schools after 30 years of service and is currently the Executive Director of *Teacher 2 Teacher* (www.teacher2teacher.info), a national educational consulting company based in Ohio. Betsy began her career as a special education teacher, eventually moving on to the regular education classroom. While in the regular classroom she worked on many cutting-edge strategies including student-led conferences and short-cycle assessments. From 2000–2007 Betsy worked in the Literacy Curriculum Alignment Project (LCAP), training over 1500 teachers in more than 60 schools. She co-authored the book *Short-Cycle Assessment: Improving Student Achievement through Formative Assessment*, which details the process developed in the LCAP work. Betsy co-authored a second book titled *Critical Thinking and Formative Assessments: Raising the Rigor in Your Classroom*, which provides strategies to teach critical thinking skills to all students. In her role with *Teacher 2 Teacher*, Betsy provides quality professional development in the areas of differentiated instruction, vertical alignment, short-cycle assessment development, and developing critical thinking skills, to name a few. Betsy lives with her husband Dave, a retired high school assistant principal, in Columbus, Ohio. She has two grown children: Amy, who lives in Hilliard, Ohio, and Bryan, who lives in Lake Elsinore, California. Also living in Temecula are Betsy's grandchildren Aria Nicole and Micah Rhys.

# Contents

# Introduction: Why Do We Need Another Book About Data?

*The goal is to transform data into information,*
*and information into insight.*
—Carly Fiorina

Data is everywhere in the world today, and we have come to rely on data for almost every decision we make. We receive data prior to political elections, we study data when applying for jobs, we use data to make decisions about where to live—we even use data to decide what type of food to buy.

In this book, the word "data" is used in the singular form, and can be understood as a mass noun or as being synonymous with "a set of data." This also complies with popular usage.

As educators, we are not exempt from the onslaught of data and, in fact, we shouldn't be. Research shows that when schools use data to guide instruction, achievement gains are made. The current experts on data and instruction state that instructional improvement depends on simple, data-driven formats—teams identifying and addressing areas of difficulty and then developing, critiquing, testing and upgrading efforts in light of ongoing results (Schmoker, 2003). A specific study by the Bay Area School Reform Collaborative revealed that schools that reviewed data several times each month were far more likely to close achievement gaps than those that reviewed data only a few times a year (Oberman & Symonds, 2005).

In the world of education we are inundated with data. The difficulty comes when we are required to analyze the data we receive, and then even more important, when we are asked to make instructional decisions about the data. This is where the problem lies.

If you are lucky enough to teach in a school where you're given the time and opportunity to analyze the data from your state tests, formative assessments, or even summative assessments, good for you. Many of us are not in that situation. We are provided the data, but often we're not given the means nor the knowledge to analyze it. Then, even if we are provided with the opportunity to discuss and look at the data, we're often not given any kind of direction as to the next step: changing our instruction. Although likely the most important step, it is also the one most ignored.

Albert Einstein said that insanity is doing the same thing over and over again while expecting different results. This is what we sometimes do in education. We give assessments and analyze our data; often we identify instructional implications related to that data; and then we continue to instruct as we have done all along.

The overriding question then becomes, "Why?"

Why would we continue to instruct students in a way that clearly shows they're not learning what we have taught? With the implementation of No Child Left Behind Act (2001) (NCLB; Public Law 107–110), we are being placed under more and more pressure to educate our students and bring them up to an expected level of achievement. In addition, students are being looked at according to a growth model in which all students, regardless of their beginning level of achievement, are expected to make one year's growth instructionally in one year's time. This makes it even more imperative that we learn how to use our data to make instructional changes that will most benefit our students.

So, the question continues to be—why are many teachers finding it so difficult to make necessary instructional changes when the data clearly show that what they're doing isn't working?

The answer to this question is fairly simple and will be addressed in detail in this book. The reason teachers don't make the instructional changes they should be making in response to the data is because they don't know what to do!

Even when teachers become adept at identifying instructional implications based on their data, they're stymied as to what steps to take to change the data. Let's look at an example. Suppose a teacher has given a short-cycle formative assessment. She's graded the assessment and analyzed the data. She's able to see very clearly from the data that the students did not perform well on the questions that required higher level, critical thinking skills. The instructional implication then becomes, "My students need to become more proficient at higher level, critical thinking skills."

Now, this is where the problem comes in: suppose that the teacher involved has never been trained in critical thinking skills or how to teach them to students? What becomes of the revelation that the students need help with this skill? Most probably, nothing—and most probably the same instructional implication will appear on subsequent data analysis. Again, if something different isn't done then different results will not magically appear!

This book is written to guide teachers to the next level—the level beyond the data. Instead of letting teachers struggle aimlessly with all the data they have to navigate, this book will detail exactly what teachers should look for in their data and what to do with what they find.

Chapter 1 provides teachers with the tools they need to compile the data in a way that is clear, concise, and open to analysis. Ways to aggregate the data will be given so that teachers can know which things to pay attention to and which things to place on the back burner. In other words, when looking at your data how do you get the biggest bang for your buck? This chapter shows you how to organize your data so that you pay attention to the correct and most important things.

Chapter 2 looks at the "what" of the data analysis puzzle. What is the data saying? What does it mean for instruction? What does it mean for professional development? What does it mean for individual students? Chapter Two looks specifically at the questions to ask when analyzing data. How will you take what you learn from the data and make sense of it? What do you need to do to change the data? This chapter provides tools to help you analyze the data and ask the hard questions that will begin the instructional change process.

Chapter 3 will move readers from the "what" to the "how." Pulling out the instructional implications is an important part of the data analyzing process, but the next step has to be getting from point A to point B. Chapter 3 deals with strategies and techniques for making goals that are not only "doable," but also will lead easily to the changes in instruction that need to be made to change the data the next time.

Delving into the "how" of going beyond the data is the intent of Chapter 4. The basic tenants of differentiation will be discussed including what it is, how to do it, and how to manage it in the classroom. Basic steps for instructional changes that will lead to flexible grouping, tiered lesson plans, and how to manage the process will be explored.

Chapter 5 gets into the specifics of the "how" with regard to the data in specific subject areas. Strategies in response to data will be examined for the subjects of reading and writing, as well as strategies for math, social studies, and science. This chapter is designed to be subject-specific with regard to data, but at the same time the strategies are ones that can be applied across grade levels and subject areas for increased student achievement.

Chapter 6 will deal specifically with higher level, critical thinking skills since the data many times reveals this to be an area that needs to be strengthened. This chapter includes what to do and how to do it with regard to higher level thinking. Strategies that can be used immediately will be provided along with opportunities to deepen understanding of not only what constitutes critical thinking, but what it looks like in the classroom.

Chapter 7 provides suggestions on how to teach test-taking skills since many times this is critical to improving the data. When analyzing data, it is important to know that the format of the test, the preparation for the test, or even the testing environment is not skewing the data. In addition, many times test-taking skills are not intentionally taught within the curriculum. This chapter will reveal how to teach these important skills to students at all grade levels.

Finally, Chapter 8 pulls all of the information together as you're provided with ways to chart the data to show improvement over time. This chapter includes strategies for teachers to use to follow the improvements in the data, and also ways for the students to keep track of their own data and thus their own improvements. As with the previous books, Blueprints for the Process will be provided at the end of the book. These will include handouts and templates to use as you begin the journey through the data.

Finally, it is important to note that the lack of follow-through with regard to data is not an issue of laziness or apathy. Teachers are extremely hard working, putting in hours and hours of their own time in order to make their students be the best they can be. The problem is that with all of the added pressures on educators today—state tests, accountability issues, the sometimes challenging behavior of students, the lack of monetary support, and especially the lack of time to do all that is needed—teachers are simply at a loss as to what to do. This book is meant to make some of these issues a little easier, for we all need to learn from each other and work together so we can continue to do what's best for kids.

# CHAPTER 1

# Compiling the Data:
## How to Make It All Make Sense

*In God we trust. All others must bring data.*
—Robert W. Hayden

## Compilation of the Data:
### Knowing What Data to Analyze

With so many fancy programs on data analysis around, there are many different options when it comes to looking at data. Before deciding on one of these programs you first need to decide *what* data to analyze. An easy place to start would be data that come to you at regular intervals throughout a school year, with time in-between to really impact instruction. That type of data may come from short-cycle assessments, content unit tests, assessment of learning targets, quizzes, or even midterm exams. It is important that you have time to analyze the data before another assessment is given, and that you have time to change something instructionally before you test again. For the sake of example, let's use short-cycle assessments. In your school these may be called *quarterly assessments* or *common assessments*, or even *benchmark assessments*. These are assessments that test certain standards that have been taught over a given amount of time. Quarterly assessments given four times a year allow a lot of time for instructional changes, but don't think that just because you're looking at quarterly data you have a whole quarter of a year to analyze it. In order for the analysis of data to be effective, it must be done quickly. Remember, old data is cold data and that means the analysis should

**Tip:** One way to determine which data to analyze is to list all your sources of data and then rank them according to which ones most impact your instruction. The # 1 ranked data should be the first one that you analyze.

be done within a couple of weeks of the administration of the assessment. A chart titled *A Practical Data Analysis Timeline*, on page 73, which describes the different timelines of the data analysis process, is included for you in the Blueprints section of this book. Basically it follows the premise that you give an assessment, you analyze the data within a set time frame, and then intentionally change something you do before you reassess at the end of the next time period.

## Compilation of the Data:
### Knowing How to Visually Represent the Data

Once you've selected the assessment data to analyze, the question becomes how to visibly organize the data so that you have the best "view" of it. Depending on how data-savvy you are this can be anything from a class profile graph to a simple data chart. The important thing is that your main piece of data is very comprehensive and holistic. In other words, you don't want your main representation to be a graph that includes many different subgroups, or categories; instead, it should be a simple chart that includes all of the student scores on one page. Figure 1.1 shows a simple data chart in which the students' names are listed as well as their scores for each test item. The scores reflect the number of points the student scored on each question. If the question is worth two points, and a "1" is placed in the box, that means the student scored one of the two points on that question. Study Figure 1.1.

According to this data chart only one student earned the maximum number of points (4) on question #5, while all of the students earned the maximum number of points (1) on question #7. Notice also that only 1 student out of 12 got all of the questions correct, while 5 out of 12 scored below 50%. Finally, notice that the percent of mastery for each item requires that the student earn both points on the 2-point questions, and 3 or 4 points on the 4-point questions to be considered true "mastery."

Figure 1.1 represents a clear, concise representation of the data. For your convenience, a blank *Assessment Data Chart* is provided for you on page 74 in the Blueprints section.

## Representing the Data:
### The Class Profile Graph

When thinking about how to compile your data sometimes the old saying "less is more" rings true. You can get so bogged down in charts and graphs that many times you lose track of what's what. If you're a person new to looking at data, then you're going to want to keep it simple. The Data Chart has

**■ Figure 1.1**
Assessment Data Chart

| Student Name | #1 1 pt. | #2 2 pts. | #3 1 pt. | #4 2 pts. | #5 4 pts. | #6 1 pt. | #7 1 pt. | #8 1 pt. | #9 2 pts | #10 1 pt. | Total Pts. | % |
|---|---|---|---|---|---|---|---|---|---|---|---|---|
| Jose | 1 | 0 | 1 | 1 | 1 | 0 | 1 | 1 | 0 | 1 | 7/16 | 44% |
| Brandon | 1 | 0 | 1 | 1 | 2 | 1 | 1 | 1 | 1 | 1 | 10/16 | 63% |
| Courtney | 1 | 2 | 1 | 1 | 3 | 1 | 1 | 1 | 1 | 1 | 13/16 | 81% |
| Heather | 0 | 1 | 0 | 1 | 0 | 0 | 1 | 1 | 0 | 1 | 5/16 | 31% |
| Brett | 1 | 2 | 1 | 1 | 2 | 1 | 1 | 1 | 1 | 0 | 11/16 | 69% |
| Alison | 1 | 1 | 1 | 1 | 1 | 1 | 1 | 1 | 1 | 1 | 10/16 | 63% |
| Michael | 0 | 0 | 0 | 1 | 2 | 1 | 1 | 1 | 0 | 1 | 7/16 | 44% |
| Cassidy | 1 | 1 | 1 | 1 | 0 | 1 | 1 | 1 | 1 | 0 | 8/16 | 50% |
| Aria | 1 | 2 | 1 | 2 | 4 | 1 | 1 | 1 | 2 | 1 | 16/16 | 100% |
| Bryan | 1 | 2 | 1 | 1 | 3 | 1 | 1 | 1 | 1 | 0 | 12/16 | 75% |
| Lisa | 1 | 2 | 1 | 1 | 2 | 1 | 1 | 1 | 1 | 1 | 12/16 | 75% |
| Dacquan | 0 | 1 | 0 | 1 | 0 | 0 | 1 | 0 | 0 | 1 | 4/16 | 25% |
| Points. Earned | 9 | 14 | 9 | 13 | 20 | 9 | 12 | 11 | 9 | 9 | | |
| Possible Points. | 12 | 24 | 12 | 24 | 48 | 12 | 12 | 12 | 24 | 12 | | |
| % Mastery | 75% | 42% | 75% | 8% | 25% | 75% | 100% | 92% | 8% | 75% | | |

everything you need to be able to analyze your data. You don't need any other graphs or charts. With that being said, sometimes it's helpful to see the data through different graphical representations.

If you're a person already familiar with looking at data, or you're a really strong visual learner, you might want to compile the data in different ways. The next logical way of looking at the data would be to take the information from the Data Chart and compile a Class Profile Graph. A Class Profile Graph is a bar graph that shows the overall percentage score for each student on that assessment. An example of a Class Profile Graph using the data from Figure 1.1 is shown in Figure 1.2 on page 4. Notice that this graph doesn't give you any information as far as the individual items. It does, however, give you an overall look at your class.

Once you have compiled your data into a Class Profile Graph, you can add different criteria to it to make it more detailed. For example, you can add a line at whatever percentage you consider to be "proficient." This has been done for the graph in Figure 1.3 on page 4.

This may be 75% or 80%—whatever you deem "mastery." You also may want to add a line at the percentage mastery for your state test; e.g., if the state cut percentile for a test is 35%, that means the students need to score

■ **Figure 1.2**  Class Profile Graph
(Overall Percentage Score for Each Student)

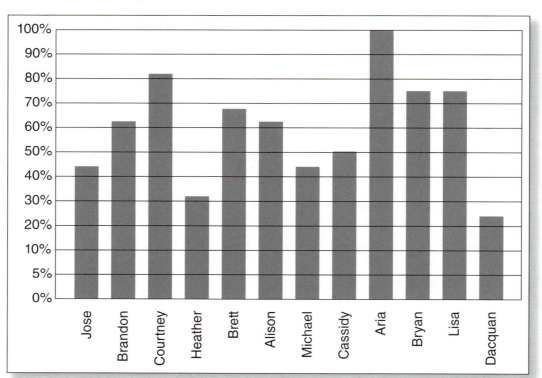

■ **Figure 1.3**  Class Mastery Graph
(Overall Percentage Score for Each Student with the Line for Mastery)

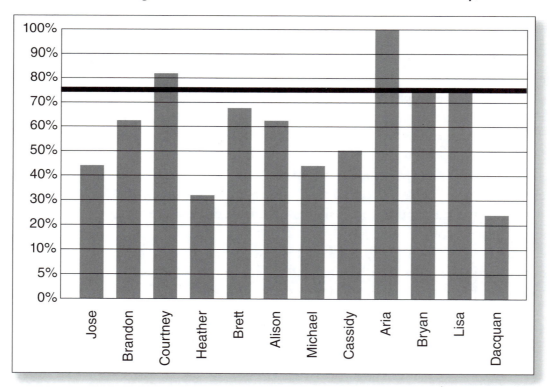

**■ Figure 1.4**  Class Cut Score Graph
(Overall Percentage Score for Each Student with the Line for Cut Score)

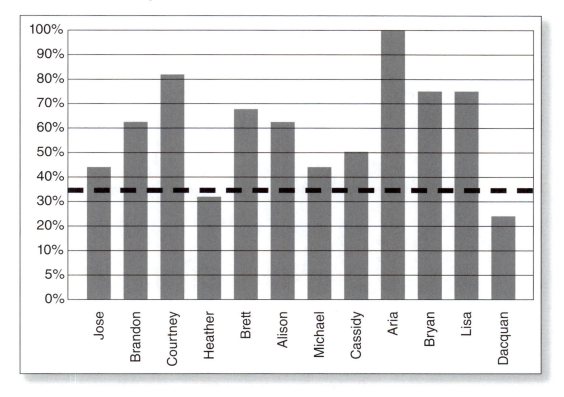

35% or above on the state test to be considered "passing." An example of a cut score graph is shown in Figure 1.4.

Another way to compile the data for a Class Profile graph would be to place both the cut percentage and the percentage considered "mastery" on the same graph. Figure 1.5 on page 6 shows what that type of graph would look like.

A logical recommendation would be that you try out different types of Class Profile Graphs and find one or two that help you best understand your data. A blank *Class Profile Graph* has been provided for you on page 75 in the Blueprints section.

**Tip:** If you choose to share this graph with parents or students, simply replace each of the student names with a number. This will help to insure anonymity.

## Representing the Data:
### The Item Analysis Graph

Many of us like to know how our students performed on individual items. The information on the Assessment Data Chart can easily be compiled into an Item Analysis Graph. An Item Analysis Graph reflecting the data from the Data Chart in Figure 1.1 is shown in Figure 1.6 on page 6.

This graph will show at a glance how the entire class performed on each individual item with regard to mastery. It will go a long way in determining

■ **Figure 1.5** Class Mastery and Cut Score Graph (Overall Percentage Score for Each Student with the Line for Mastery and the Line for the Cut Score )

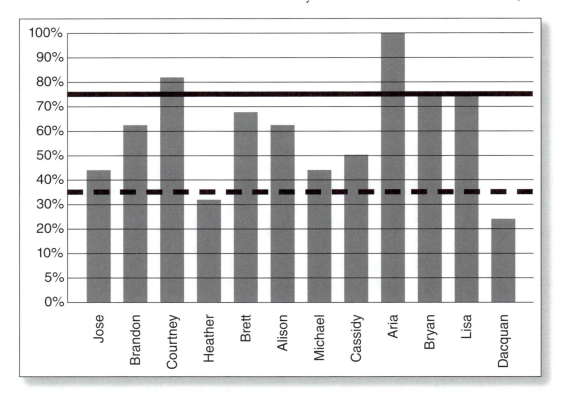

■ **Figure 1.6** Item Analysis Graph
(Percentage of Class for Mastery of Each Item )

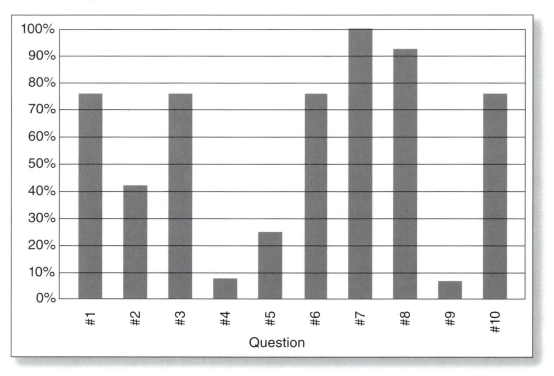

*I Have the Data...Now What?*

the format of the questions the class is struggling with, as well as the individual standards or even the level of questions that are posing problems for the students. As with the Class Profile Graph, you can draw a "mastery" line and/or a cut score line horizontally to show how the class performed with regard to those two criteria.

To help you compile the data, see the blank *Item Analysis Graph* on page 76 in the Blueprints section.

**Tip:** If you want to compare "like" items, simply place those items next to one another on the item analysis graph. Examples of "like" items might be ones that assess specific standards or items whose formats are the same, etc.

## Keeping the Data Simple

No matter which way you choose to compile your data, the questions you ask should be the same. Again, if you have only one representation of the data, the Data Chart, you will have everything you need for analysis. The other graphs will certainly enhance your understanding of the data, but they're not necessary. Now, what exactly does that mean? Well, take for example the Data Chart in Figure 1.1. By simply highlighting each box in which the student achieved mastery for an item, you can visually see all of the data and trends that you can see with fancy graphs. This has been done for you in Figure 1.7.

■ **Figure 1.7**  Highlighted Data Chart
(Items Highlighted Show Items of Mastery)

| Student Name | #1 1 pt. | #2 2 pts. | #3 1 pt. | #4 2 pts. | #5 4 pts. | #6 1 pt. | #7 1 pt. | #8 1 pt. | #9 2 pts | #10 1 pt. | Total Pts. | % |
|---|---|---|---|---|---|---|---|---|---|---|---|---|
| Jose | 1 | 0 | 1 | 1 | 1 | 0 | 1 | 1 | 0 | 1 | 7/16 | 44% |
| Brandon | 1 | 0 | 1 | 1 | 2 | 1 | 1 | 1 | 1 | 1 | 10/16 | 63% |
| Courtney | 1 | 2 | 1 | 1 | 3 | 1 | 1 | 1 | 1 | 1 | 13/16 | 81% |
| Heather | 0 | 1 | 0 | 1 | 0 | 0 | 1 | 1 | 0 | 1 | 5/16 | 31% |
| Brett | 1 | 2 | 1 | 1 | 2 | 1 | 1 | 1 | 1 | 0 | 11/16 | 69% |
| Alison | 1 | 1 | 1 | 1 | 1 | 1 | 1 | 1 | 1 | 1 | 10/16 | 63% |
| Michael | 0 | 0 | 0 | 1 | 2 | 1 | 1 | 1 | 0 | 1 | 7/16 | 44% |
| Cassidy | 1 | 1 | 1 | 1 | 0 | 1 | 1 | 1 | 1 | 0 | 8/16 | 50% |
| Aria | 1 | 2 | 1 | 2 | 4 | 1 | 1 | 1 | 2 | 1 | 16/16 | 100% |
| Bryan | 1 | 2 | 1 | 1 | 3 | 1 | 1 | 1 | 1 | 0 | 12/16 | 75% |
| Lisa | 1 | 2 | 1 | 1 | 2 | 1 | 1 | 1 | 1 | 1 | 12/16 | 75% |
| Dacquan | 0 | 1 | 0 | 1 | 0 | 0 | 1 | 0 | 0 | 1 | 4/16 | 25% |
| Points. Earned | 9 | 14 | 9 | 13 | 20 | 9 | 12 | 11 | 9 | 9 | | |
| Possible Points. | 12 | 24 | 12 | 24 | 48 | 12 | 12 | 12 | 24 | 12 | | |
| % Mastery | 75% | 42% | 75% | 8% | 25% | 75% | 100% | 92% | 8% | 75% | | |

This chart has now been configured to let you see at a glance both the achievement of individual students and the success, or lack thereof, of individual items. Looking across horizontally you can determine which students may need enrichment, and which students may need remediation. Likewise, if you look vertically at the columns you can see which items the students were the most successful with, and on which items the students struggled. This is a simple, clear and concise way to look at the data. You only need one chart and a highlighter.

## Housing the Data

Many times the most difficult part of analyzing the data is actually finding the data. Data come to us in all formats, colors, shapes and sizes. Keeping all of your data in one place will help you to keep your data organized. Usually all this takes is a three-ring binder. You can make a "Data Notebook" for all of your important data. Using subject dividers to clearly label the data will also aid in the organization process. Once you have your data compiled in one place remember to keep it close by, especially as you plan for instruction. A data file cabinet or data folders can serve the same purpose as a data notebook, although either one of these choices may not be as portable or organized as you want.

## A Final Word on Data Compilation

Keep in mind that these graphs can be created by hand, or electronically. You can choose to create them yourself or you can choose a program to create them for you. There is no right or wrong way to compile the data. You have to find out the most comfortable and manageable way for you—and it should be your choice. Too many times data is given to us in formats that are unfamiliar and many times, well, confusing and even scary! Taken down to the basics, compiling data is really an easy thing to do.

# CHAPTER 2

# Analyzing the Data:
# What Does It All Mean?

*It is the mark of an educated mind to be able to entertain
a thought without accepting it.*

—Aristotle

## What Is Analysis Anyway???

Twenty-five years ago the world of data was restricted mostly to school psychologists, special educators, and speech teachers. Most of us operated according to what we *thought* was best for kids, and we were pretty much left alone. All that changed in the 1990's and especially into the 21st century as we came into the age of standards-based learning and high-stakes testing. All of a sudden it wasn't about what *we* thought was best, but what the data was telling us was best. That would be alright if we had been adequately trained to analyze data and knew exactly what to do with it. But many of us were not. We were given lots of data, sure, and even taught to use data software. We learned how to print out impressive graphs on our students and even became fairly adept at drawing conclusions from these graphs. Most of the time, however, our learning was purely superficial. We learned the basics of data analysis; that is, we were able to pull out the most obvious parts of the data. But, we were never taught to actually *analyze* the data.

The ability to analyze something requires using critical, higher level thinking skills. The definition of the level of Analysis according to Bloom's Taxonomy is to "examine and break information into parts by identifying motives and causes; to make inferences and find evidence to support generalizations" (Barton, 1997). That means that in order to really analyze data we have to be able to take them apart and scrutinize all the parts. We also have to be able to come to conclusions by inferring, or in other words, by making decisions when things are not specifically spelled out for us. That becomes very difficult for many of us for two reasons; first, we haven't been trained *how* to analyze, and second, analysis takes time, and time is something we never have enough of.

## Data Analysis Process: Six Steps

Analysis of data is a skill that takes practice, but it is something that can be done once you understand the steps to doing it. To make it simple, the data analysis process has been divided into six steps. They are:

**Step 1:** Displaying the Data in a User-Friendly Way

**Step 2:** Asking Questions about the Data

**Step 3:** Answering Questions Generated from the Data

**Step 4:** Forming Instructional Implications Implied by the Data

**Step 5:** Making Goals to Change the Results of the Data

**Step 6:** Knowing How to Assess the Goals

The first three steps of this process will be examined in this chapter. The final three steps comprise the "how" of going beyond the data and will be examined in detail in Chapters 3 and 4.

### Step 1: Displaying the Data in a User-Friendly Way

The first step when it comes to analyzing data is to display it in a way that is easy to read and understand. The information provided in Chapter 1 details how to do this in a way that is concise and clear. The important thing to consider when compiling the data is very simple—what is it that you want to examine? Let's say that I am a middle school math teacher and I have just been to a conference regarding gender bias and the teaching of math. I am interested in seeing if there is a difference in the way the girls in my math classes perform as opposed to the boys. I would need to compile the data in such a way that I could clearly view what it is I want to know. Therefore, I'd probably aggregate my data so that I had different sections of the graph for the scores of the girls in my class and for the boys in my class. For example, I'd compile a class profile graph in which the girl's scores were on one side and the boy's scores were on the other side. An example of this is shown in Figure 2.1.

Likewise, as I compile the item analysis scores for this assessment, I'd compile it in such a way that would allow me to compare the way the girls scored on each item to the way that the boys scored. An example of an item analysis graph aggregated this way is shown in Figure 2.2.

**■ Figure 2.1** Class Profile Graph Aggregated by Gender
Scores for Math Assessment #2

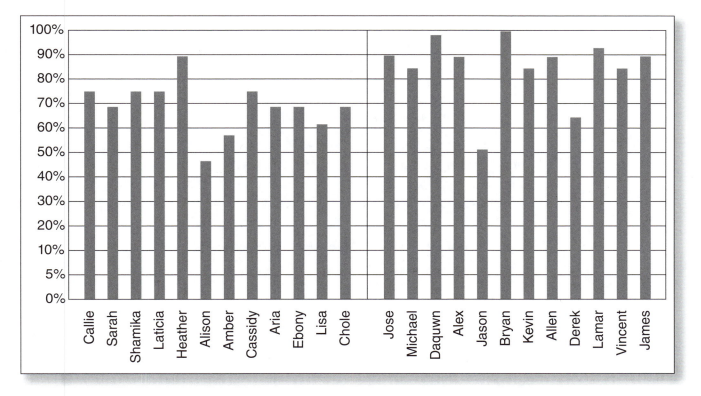

**■ Figure 2.2** Classroom Item Analysis Graph Aggregated by Gender
Scores for Math Assessment #2

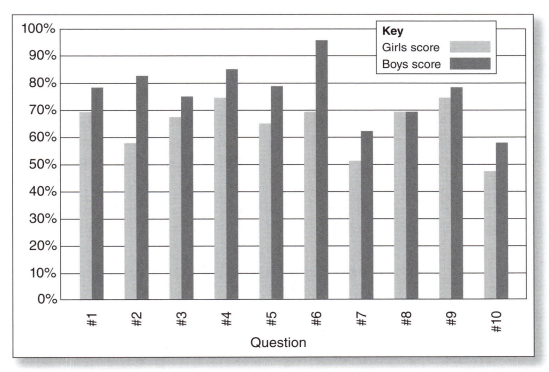

**Tip:** One way to determine what it is you want most to learn from your data is to ask yourself the following question: "If I could find out one thing from analyzing this data, what would I want to know?" Ask this question prior to any analysis of the data.

The most important questions to ask in regard to the compilation of the data are "What do I want to know?" or "What am I trying to find out?" It is imperative that there be a very specific goal in the compilation of the data and this should be determined ahead of time. Too many times data is provided to teachers without a specific purpose in mind. Being mindful of the *objective* of the data is the first step in successful analysis of the data.

## Step 2: Asking Questions about the Data

Once the data has been compiled toward a specific central question, other detail questions need to be asked and answered in order to relevantly examine the data. This can be done by objectively viewing the data while brainstorming various questions about it. There are several criteria to use when generating questions about data:

♦ Look for data that does not make sense.

♦ Look for data that ties directly to student achievement.

♦ Look for data that demonstrates trends over time.

♦ Look for data that will lead to changes in instruction.

Keeping in mind the criteria for generating questions about the data, begin the construction of the questions. For your convenience, see the template, *Questions Related to the Data,* on page 77 in the Blueprints section. Some questions that could be generated when looking at the data in Figures 2.1 and 2.2 can be found in Figure 2.3. Study the questions in Figure 2.3.

These questions can now serve as a springboard to look at what to do with the data. A couple of other points need to be made about generating

■ **Figure 2.3**    Questions Related to the Data
Questions Generated for Math Assessment #2

---

♦ Was there a difference between the scores of the boys and the scores of the girls? What does this mean?

♦ What was the class mean for this assessment? What was the mean for the girls? For the boys?

♦ Were there any struggling students who did better than expected? Were there any competent students who did not do as well as you expected?

♦ Were there certain standards on which the girls were stronger than the boys? The boys stronger than the girls?

♦ Were there certain types of questions on which the girls scored better than the boys? Were there certain types of questions on which both groups struggled?

♦ How was the instruction delivered? Is there any research on whether one type of instruction is better for girls? For boys? What does that mean for the classroom?

---

questions about data. First of all, it's essential to stay completely unbiased when generating the questions. Teachers may need to step outside of the box as they look at things that seem odd about their results. This can be compared to a CSI investigator examining a crime scene. Another important point to keep in mind is that the analysis of the data, beginning with the generation of questions, needs to be done in a timely manner. Remember, old data is cold data. When looking at data, either for a formative short-cycle assessment, a unit test, or even an authentic assessment, the analysis should be done within a week or two of administration.

### Step 3: Answering Questions Generated from the Data

After generating questions related to the data, the next step in the data analysis process is to answer the questions. An easy way to organize your questions is to put them into categories according to the topic for which you want more information. The topic for the above example might be "Gender Differences in Achievement." It is important to note that as a teacher, you may be looking at multiple categories with regard to the data. For example, let's say that in addition to the gender differences, as a teacher you also want to examine how your students are doing with regard to higher level critical thinking questions. You can generate questions and answers to both topics at one time thus allowing you to analyze two different aspects of the data. A tool for the compilation of the questions and answers might look like the sample in Figure 2.4 on page 14.

A blank copy of this tool, *Classification of Questions and Answers from the Data Chart*, is provided on page 78 in the Blueprints section.

Keep in mind that at this point in the process, the goal is not to solve the problem. It's important to keep a focus on this. The reason for this is that by going through the process step-by-step, you will retain the objectivity of the analysis. Too often in education we look for a "quick fix" and that sometimes involves changing the assessment process to change the data instead of changing instructional practices to change the data. By staying with the process the objectivity of the process will be maintained and the students will be the better for it.

**Tip:** Write the question that you are attempting to answer at the top of the page of data. For example: "Was there any difference in the scores of the girls versus the boys on this assessment?" This will help you to remember your point of reference when you analyzed the data.

## A Final Word on the Meaning of the Data

When analyzing the data it is important to stick with a specific process. Most of us weren't taught how to analyze data, we were simply given the data and expected to know what it meant. A six-step process for analyzing data has been provided. The first step is compiling the data according to a specific criteria—what is it you want to know? The second step is generating questions related to the data and to your criteria. These questions should

**■ Figure 2.4**   Classification of Questions and Answers from the Data

| Topic | Question | Answer |
|---|---|---|
| Gender Differences in Achievement | Was there a difference in the scores of the girls and the scores of the boys on this assessment? What does that mean? | Yes, there was a difference. The boys scored higher. This could mean that the boys are able to think more abstractly than the girls. It could also mean that the boys are able to learn more efficiently with the way the subject is now being taught. |
| Gender Differences in Achievement | What was the class mean for this assessment? What was the mean for the girls? For the boys? | The class mean was 70%. The mean for the girls was 65% while the mean for the boys was 75%. |
| Gender Differences in Achievement | Were there certain types of questions on which the girls scored better than the boys? Were there certain types of questions on which both groups struggled? | The girls scored better on the constructed-response questions in which they had to explain their answers. Both groups struggled with the critical thinking questions. |
| Critical Thinking Skills | Were the students successful on the questions that required critical thinking? What does this mean? | No, the students as a whole were not successful on the higher level, critical thinking questions. This means that more instruction in this area is needed. |
| Critical Thinking Skills | Was there one specific level of Bloom's Taxonomy on which the students were the least successful? The most successful? | The students were the least successful on the questions involving synthesis. The students were the most successful on the questions involving evaluation. |

be brainstormed according to what looks strange in the data. Remember to keep a focused approach. Pretend you are an investigator investigating an occurrence. The third step in the process is answering the generated questions. It's important during this step not to try to solve the problems that will be inferred. You simply want to answer the questions to the best of your knowledge according to the data that you have.

The ability to analyze the data objectively is imperative to the future success of your students. Therefore, it is recommended that you go through the steps of the analysis process in order to maintain that objectivity. The ironic thing is that the more objective you can be, the more information you'll get which will allow you to be more subjective as you make instructional decisions related to your students. This will allow you to not only increase the achievement of your students, but to increase your proficiency as a teacher.

# CHAPTER 3

# Analyzing the Data:
## What to Do About It

*Always have a plan, and believe in it. Nothing happens by accident.*
—Chuck Knox

## Identifying Instructional Goals

Data analysis can be a simple process if you divide it into parts. Going through a simple, six-step process for analyzing data can make it not only easy to understand, but also informative and thought provoking. For the ease of any teacher analyzing data, this six-step process is as follows:

**Step 1:** Displaying the Data in a User-Friendly Way

**Step 2:** Asking Questions about the Data

**Step 3:** Answering Questions Generated from the Data

**Step 4:** Forming Instructional Implications Implied by the Data

**Step 5:** Making Goals to Change the Results of the Data

**Step 6:** Knowing How to Assess the Goals

The first three steps in this process were described in detail in Chapter 2. In this chapter, the last three steps will be examined. These three steps are: forming instructional implications implied by the data, making goals to change the results of the data, and knowing how to assess those goals.

The next obvious step in this process is to pull out the instructional implications that have presented themselves based on the data. These instructional implications will be generated both by the informal analysis of the data as teachers look at them initially and by the intentional analysis of the data as they create their questions related to the data.

### Step 4: Forming Instructional Implications Implied by the Data

There are several ways to determine the instructional implications for the data being analyzed. One is to simply brainstorm thoughts that occur as the data are examined. This would culminate in a list and could be created by one teacher or by a common group of teachers—say subject area or grade level teachers. When looking for instructional implications, look for things that present themselves naturally following the asking and answering of questions in steps 2 and 3. Figure 3.1 is an example of this type of list.

Another way to determine instructional implications based on the data may come from specific worksheets or tools that will better define the issues. Two types of these tools are shown in Figures 3.2 and 3.3. Each one asks either a single teacher or a group of teachers to analyze the data and come up with instructional implications. Notice that these tools require a lot more attention to detail than the brainstormed list. They are all good tools to use to get to the implications for instruction; it may simply be a matter of what works best for you. Also, it is important to change the way you analyze the data over time, so you may opt to use different tools each time. That serves to keep the analysis process fresh. Both of these tools, *Data Analysis Instructional Implications Chart #1 and Chart #2*, are provided for you on pages 79 and 80 in the Blueprints section.

One thing that is very interesting about this analysis is that many of the instructional implications do not deal with the content area, but rather

■ **Figure 3.1**  Brainstormed List of Instructional Implications

---

**Math Assessment # 2 – Instructional Implications**

♦ Students need to improve their skill in writing constructed-response-question answers.

♦ Students need to improve their ability to think at higher critical thinking levels.

♦ Students need to improve their ability to problem solve.

♦ Students need to strengthen their knowledge of the basic math facts.

♦ Strategies and techniques need to be implemented to increase gender issues in the classroom.

♦ Test-taking skills need to be strengthened.

♦ The ability to understand what a question is asking needs to be strengthened.

---

| Ques. | Standard | Ques. Type | Ques. Level | Student Performance | Instructional Implication |
|---|---|---|---|---|---|
| Key: MC: Multiple Choice CR: Constructed Response RG: Response Grid | | | | | |
| 1 | #4 | MC | Lower | Excellent | ◆ The skill "order of operations" has been mastered. Less time can be spent instructing this skill. |
| 2 | #3 | CR | Higher | Poor | ◆ Students need more instruction on rational numbers.<br>◆ Students need to improve their ability to write answers to constructed-response questions.<br>◆ Students need to strengthen their critical-thinking skills. |
| 3 | #8 | RG | Lower | Poor | ◆ Students need review of basic division using two divisors.<br>◆ Students need to practice answering response-grid questions. |
| 4 | # 10 | MC | Higher | Fair | ◆ Flexible groups need to be used to address the differences in performance for multiplication of two-digit numbers. |

■ **Figure 3.3**   Data Analysis Instructional Implications Chart #2

Key: MC: Multiple Choice CR: Constructed Response RG: Response Grid
HL: Higher Level LL: Lower Level

| Most Successful | | | | | | | Least Successful | | | | | | |
|---|---|---|---|---|---|---|---|---|---|---|---|---|---|
| Ques. | Standard | MC | CR | RG | HL | LL | Ques. | Standard | MC | CR | RG | HL | LL |
| 1 | #2 | X | | | | X | 2 | #6 | | X | | X | |
| 5 | #4 | X | | | | X | 4 | #5 | | | X | | X |
| 8 | #2 | X | | | | X | 6 | #6 | | X | | X | |
| 10 | #4 | | X | | | X | 13 | #6 | X | | | X | |
| 12 | #4 | X | | | | X | 14 | #8 | | X | | | X |

### Instructional Implications:

◆ Students did very well on multiple choice, lower level questions. I need to provide practice with higher levels of Bloom's.

◆ Students did very well on Standard # 4: Identify fact and opinion. I can spend less instructional time on this skill.

◆ Students struggled with constructed-response questions. I need to provide more practice in this skill.

◆ Students struggled with higher level questions. I need to provide more practice in these skills.

◆ Students struggled with response-grid questions. I need to show students how to answer these types of questions and provide more practice with them.

test-taking skills. If no analysis were done on this assessment, the assumption may have been made that the students were deficient in certain standards when in fact it's the format of the test that's troubling them. This discovery is very important for a teacher as further instruction is planned and carried out.

## Step 5: Making Goals to Change the Results of the Data

Once instructional implications have been pulled from the data, it is essential that some sort of goal be developed to get to the "how" of the implication. If this important step is left out of the data analysis process, then the same instructional implications will continue to appear time and time again in subsequent data. As suggested before, as you come to this step in the process, it's recommended that you keep it simple. Consider making only one or two goals at first. These goals should be specifically aligned to the instructional implications. They also need to be time sensitive and measurable. There are many types of action plans available today, but again, some of these can be quite intimidating. A simple way to develop a goal related to the data is to simply add it on to whatever tool you use for your instructional implications. If you're brainstorming, either individually or in a group, you could simply create a list to be placed next to your instructional implications list that was already developed. That might look like the two charts in Figure 3.4.

If you want to use an Action Plan, you might consider a very simple one such as the one shown in Figure 3.5.

For your convenience, several different types of *Action Plans* can be found on pages 81–83 in the Blueprints section. When making goals based on instructional implications, you can use different plans at different times to keep the process fresh.

When you are writing goals, it is important that you make them very specific and measurable. There are four specific steps to creating a goal:

1. Ask questions about the data.

2. Answer the questions.

■ **Figure 3.4**   Goals from Brainstormed List of Instructional Implications

| Instructional Implications | Instructional Goals |
|---|---|
| ♦ Students need to strengthen their ability to answer constructed response questions. | ♦ Students will write in a Math Journal once a week and explain how they got the answer to a given problem. |
| ♦ Students need to strengthen their recall of the basic multiplication facts. | ♦ Students needing practice will work on  multiplication fact drill programs on the computer. |

| Instructional Implication | Goal | Strategy |
|---|---|---|
| Students need to strengthen their ability to answer constructed-response questions. | Students will practice writing answers to questions by explaining how they got their answers to basic math problems. | Once a week students will be given a math problem to solve. They will then write in their Math Journal explaining how they solved the problem using words. |

**3.** Develop instructional implications from the questions and answers.

**4.** Write goals based on the instructional implications, making sure they are specific and measurable.

If you are a visual learner, the flowchart, Figure 3.6, might make more sense to you.

An example of a completed flowchart is shown in Figure 3.7 on page 20 using the information regarding constructed-response questions found previously in this chapter.

Specific goals mean very detailed goals. The more detailed you can get, the better it will be. For example, rather than stating a goal as "Students will become better at critical thinking" you would want to say, "Students will increase their ability to use analysis skills as they problem solve." Likewise, rather than stating a goal as "Students will demonstrate increased skill in

■ **Figure 3.6** Flowchart: Four Specific Steps to Creating a Goal

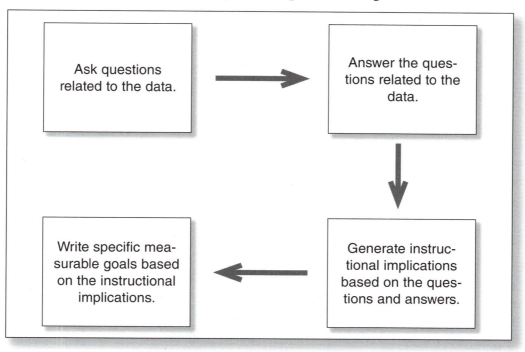

■ **Figure 3.7** Flow Chart: Writing Goals for Constructed-Response Performance

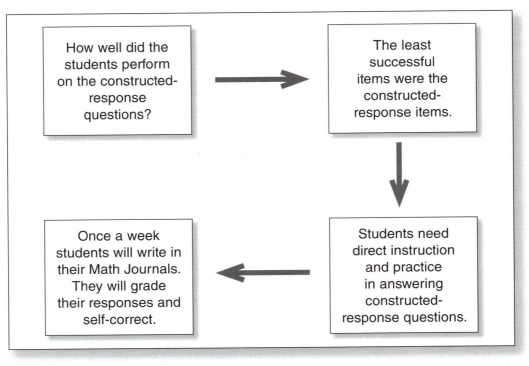

basic facts" you might say "Students will increase their skills in the basic multiplication facts through the 10's." These detailed goals will lead to more defined and exact results.

**Tip:** Whichever tool you use to make your goals, make sure that you include a copy of it with the data in your data notebook. This will be especially important as you analyze whether or not your goals were met.

## Step 6: Knowing How to Assess the Goals

The measurable component of the goals is perhaps the most important part of making goals. It's kind of like the assessing part of instruction. Many times teachers will say that they spend so much time testing that they don't have time to teach. The point that needs to be made when a statement such as this is voiced is, If you don't assess, how will you know the student learned what it is that has been taught? There is a big difference between teaching and learning and likewise there is a big difference between setting a goal and reaching a goal. The measurable part of the goal will assure you that the goal has been met. It is important to think about exactly what it is that you, as the teacher, need to see as evidence that the student, or the class, has met the goal. For example, the aforementioned goal concerning critical thinking skills was, "Students will increase their ability to use analysis skills as they problem solve." Add to that a measurable indicator, and the goal might read, "Students will increase their ability to use analysis skills as they problem solve. Each week students will receive instruction and learn strategies on how to analyze material. Eighty percent of the class will show mastery on weekly

*I Have the Data...Now What?*

problem solving activities that require them to use analysis skills." Writing a goal in this manner gives the teacher a specific plan on how to reach the goal. It's much more definable than simply the instructional implication of "Students need to improve their critical thinking skills."

One concern when looking at making goals of this nature is the element of time. Teachers are already pressed for time and this type of goal setting takes even more time. Yet, when looked at closely, making goals of this nature based on the data will actually give the teacher more "bang for a buck" and thereby lead to better time management. The goals will be so clear and succinct that the teacher will be able to efficiently instruct and then measure whether learning has taken place. In addition, the goals that are developed may be developed for specific groups only. Instead of reteaching the multiplication facts to all of the students (a clear waste of time for the students who have demonstrated mastery), it would be more efficient to reteach only those students who need the skill while the others are delving deeper into the skills or even extending beyond the skill. Take for example the goal for basic multiplication facts. The goal might be stated as a two-tiered goal that looks something like this:

> Students in Group 1 who have shown nonmastery of basic multiplication facts through the 10's will increase their skills by drilling the facts three times a week on the computer for 30 minutes at a time, and then scoring at least 85% on a 5-minute timed test given at the end of each week. Students in Group 2 who have shown mastery of basic multiplication facts through the 10's will work on problem solving activities that require them to apply the knowledge of the facts three times a week on the computer for 30 minutes at a time, scoring at least 85% on each of these tasks.

One way of getting to the specificity needed to complete these goals is to use a tool called a Goal Reaching Chart. This chart helps to delineate exactly the behaviors and evidence needed to show mastery for specific goals. An example of this chart is shown in Figure 3.8 on page 22.

A blank *Goal Reaching Chart* can be found on page 84 in the Blueprints section.

**Tip:** Use staff meetings for data analysis. This means that announcements and other managerial tasks will need to be done in a different way—perhaps through email or announcements. This should be decided on ahead of time and agreed to by all.

## A Final Word on Deciding What to Do

When making decisions regarding data, it is important to be very intentional. Developing instructional implications should come fairly naturally once the questions have been generated from the data and those questions have been answered. This is where data analysis often stops. It's important to move from the instructional implications to the setting of specific goals.

**■ Figure 3.8**   Goal Reaching Chart

| Goal | Evidence (What will you see?) | Evidence (What will you see?) | Evidence (What will you see?) |
|---|---|---|---|
| Students will show mastery of basic multiplication facts through the 10's. | Students will be able to score at least 85% on a 5-minute timed test. | Students will be able to use multiplication skills accurately when solving word problems. | Students will be able to solve two digit by two digit multiplication problems without miscalculating the basic facts. |
| Students will extend their knowledge of basic multiplication facts through the 10's. | 85% of students will be able to use multiplication skills accurately when solving word problems and explain what multiplication means. | Students will be able to solve two digit by three digit multiplication problems without miscalculating the basic facts. | Students will be able to learn and show evidence of learning (85% on timed tests) division facts. |

These goals should be as detailed as possible to add clarity to the process. The goals must also be measurable in ways that will align with the gaps in the data. Deciding what to do about the data analyzed is important; knowing exactly how to do what needs to be done is the piece of the puzzle that is often mystifying and frequently absent. The following chapters will deal with the "how" of the data analysis process. Remember, data without action will lead to doing more of the same thing.

# CHAPTER 4

# Following Data Analysis:
## Deciding How to Do What Needs to Be Done

*Education is not the piling on of learning, information, data,*
*facts, skills, or abilities—that's training or instruction—*
*but is rather making visible what is hidden as a seed.*

—Sir Thomas More

## Time to Plan for Instruction Based on the Data

Following the development of specific goals based on instructional implications, the overriding question becomes "Okay, now that I know what to do, how do I do it?" This seems like such a simple question to ask, yet in education many times this is where the data analysis process stops. Educators will make the leap from the data to instruction on paper, even to the point of making very specific goals, yet the path to get from point A to point B is often missing or never attempted. This is a result of a couple of different things. First of all, we don't always have the time to plan for instruction based on the data, and even more important, we many times don't know what to do. The information in this chapter will help solve some of the mystery.

Planning for instruction following the analysis of the data, pulling instructional implications and making instructional plans based on the data, takes a lot of time. One of the ways to allow for time to plan for personalized data instruction is to use common planning time. Common planning time occurs when teachers of the same grade level/subject area are all given the same planning time during the school day. It needs to be a time that is purposefully used for collaboration and planning. There should be specific agendas for the time (formal or informal), and there should be accountability within the group. It's during these common planning times that data should be reviewed, goals should be revisited, and plans for instruction should be made. Too many times we teachers use our planning time for managerial tasks, such as copying worksheets, returning parent calls, or dealing with discipline problems. The common planning time should be designated for planning instruction only. The group needs to be committed to this, and there should be definite steps for follow-up. Of course, this can be a problem if the only time a teacher has is the common time. When then, are the managerial tasks taken care of? The perfect situation would be one in which every teacher has common planning time in addition to a class period or time when the managerial tasks can be managed. This isn't always possible. If the only time allotted to teachers is the common planning time, then the teachers have to decide when to do the other things that need to be taken care of in the course of the day. Before school, after school, or lunch time are all possibilities, but not very attractive ones. Perhaps deciding to devote every other day to managerial tasks is the answer. It's not an easy problem to solve, but devoting planning time to deciding on instruction based on the data is something that will make a difference in the achievement of your students—something that is far more important when looking at the bigger picture.

**Tip:** Use staff meetings for data analysis. This means that announcements and other managerial tasks will need to be done in a different way—perhaps through email or announcements. This should be decided on ahead of time and agreed to by all.

## Changing Instruction Based on the Data:
### Seven Steps for Instructional Change

The second reason analyzing data doesn't always result in a change in instruction is simply because, while teachers can determine *what* to do, they sometimes don't know *how* to do it. In today's educational world we talk about differentiating instruction. Teachers will ask, "Well, now that I have the data, what do I do?" and the answer is always, "Why, you differentiate your instruction." At this point, many times those of us told to differentiate say, "Oh…okay." The missing piece to this puzzle is that it isn't always clear how to differentiate. Differentiation really isn't a product, it's a process. There isn't a ready-made kit that you can give someone with regard to differentiation. It is really about changing instruction based on what the data is telling you. A simple seven-step process is provided here to assist with the instructional changes. This process is called "Seven Steps for Instructional Change." The steps are listed in Figure 4.1. Each step will be explained in detail.

First of all, to really change instruction, you need to do something different. Too many times what we do is give the students more of the same. If the data shows that many of the students do not know their multiplication facts, what we often do is pull those students out and have them do more of what the entire class did to learn the facts. Doing the same thing will only

**■ Figure 4.1**    Seven Steps for Instructional Change

---

**Seven Steps for Instructional Change**

**Step 1:**  Determine the area of instructional change.

**Step 2:**  Determine ways to instruct the areas that are different from the original mode of instruction.

**Step 3:**  Determine the groups for instruction.

**Step 4:**  Determine what instructional strategies will be used for each group, including details of what, how, where, and when.

**Step 5:**  Determine how you will assess the learning.

**Step 6:**  Determine what you will do in reaction to the information from the assessment.

**Step 7:**  Determine how you will display the data to show if the instructional changes were effective.

---

get the same results. That means that the first thing you need to do after analyzing the data is to be committed to doing something different with your instruction. To do that you may need to do some research. You may need to read books that explain a different way to teach what you are trying to teach, or attend a conference on different instructional strategies that you may want to use. You may want to meet with several of your colleagues and "pick their brains" for different ideas, or appeal to your instructional leader or curriculum coordinator to search for new strategies for you to employ in your classroom. That means that step 1 of Instructional Change is to identify the topic/skill/content for which instruction needs to be changed, while step 2 is to find a different way to teach that topic/skill/content.

Let's go back to the multiplication example. Step 1 would have been analyzing the data and coming to the conclusion that many of the students missed questions on which they had to rely on knowing the multiplication facts. At the same time the data reveals that many of the students have already mastered the facts and performed very well on those questions that involved using the facts. That leads to the natural conclusion that this is an area in which instruction needs to be changed if future data is to change. Step 2 of the Instructional Change process, then, is finding instructional strategies different from the ones initially used. Suppose that the instructional strategy included having the students write out a multiplication matrix and then assigning certain families of facts to be memorized each week. While this strategy worked for some of the students, it obviously did not work for all students. That leads to a quest to find different ways to teach memorization of the multiplication facts for those students who did not master them. Different strategies should be brainstormed and researched at this time. Strategies might be any of these:

- Saying the facts into a tape recorder and then listening back to them over and over
- Learning or making up a song about the multiplication facts
- Playing computer games which teach the multiplication facts
- Drawing pictures with the facts in them
- Making up a multiplication rap with different rhymes and rhythms
- Making multiplication puzzles within groups and then sharing the puzzles

At the same time, ways to instruct the students who have already mastered the facts need to be implemented so that they can deepen their understanding of the multiplication process. The following strategies might be considered:

- Working on problem solving activities that require multiplication knowledge
- Writing problems for one another to solve that require using the multiplication process
- Giving the students one way to solve a multiplication problem and asking them to come up with a different way to solve the same problem
- Writing multiplication riddles in which students embed the multiple facts in riddles for each other to solve
- Developing a multiplication game in which the multiplication process must be used to win the game

Now comes the point in the Instructional Change process where the groups need to be determined. This is step 3. Using the data, decide on the criteria or even a cut score to divide the students into groups. For the multiplication example, it might be decided that any student who scored below 75% on the multiplication problems would be in the group that needs to continue to work on mastery of the facts, while the students scoring above 75% would be in the extension group. Keep in mind that these groups are flexible groups and are based on the data and not on ability. These groups may change; as soon as a student demonstrates mastery in the "working" group, the student may move to the "extension" group. In this case the decision has been made to have two groups; if a third group were added, it might be one in which the students still do not have a basic understanding of numbers and need to be taken back to the point where they are working with and understanding numbers as they relate to the concept of multiplication. That will be determined by what the data shows. The important thing to remember is that there is no one formula for deciding on groups; it is somewhat subjective based on the analysis of the data. Remember, you want to take an approach to intentionally change instruction following the analysis of the data.

After the groups have been determined, the implementation of new instructional strategies needs to occur. This is step 4 of the Instructional

**Tip:** Whenever possible, pair up with a colleague to share the workload. For example, one teacher might plan a remediation activity while the other plans the extension activity. Groups can also be divided up this way: one teacher can teach the remedial lesson, while the other one teaches the enrichment lesson.

**Tip:** Differentiated instruction is not individualized instruction. You should only have 2 to 3 flexible groups in your classroom at a time. More groups than three will be difficult to monitor and manage.

Change process. This includes exactly what will be done and how it will be done. Consideration of timelines and physical strategies such as the classroom environment should be taken into account. This is where you want to get as specific as you can. For example, using the multiplication scenario, it might be determined that three days of math instruction time will be spent, with two separate groups being instructed. Group 1 will work on memorizing the multiplication facts by working on computer games, while Group 2 will work on creating and developing multiplication games in which players need to use multiplication skills to win. At this time it will be decided which computer games to use, where the students will play them (in the classroom or in a computer lab), what materials the extension group will need to make their games, and the rubric for making the games. This is where all the details of the instructional plan are decided.

Step 5 of the Instructional Change process has to do with assessment. Assessment is going to generate the data that will show whether or not the changes in instruction were successful. This assessment should be somewhat summative in that you want to determine if what you have done has worked. The assessment for the block of lessons on multiplication might be a timed multiplication test for the group working on the facts, and grading the projects according to the rubrics for the group working on the multiplication games.

Following assessment, a plan needs to be made for further intervention and extension according to what the new data shows you. This is step 6 of the Instructional Change process. If some of the students in the math class continue to need intervention, and there is no more class time in which to learn multiplication facts, the plan might be to set up tutoring sessions after school. For those students who are ready to go beyond the basic facts, homework in which the students choose from several different projects such as making up a multiplication song or rap, or creating a multiplication puzzle, for example, might be assigned.

The final step in the Instructional Change process, step 7, is recording the data for the process. Staying with the multiplication example, a line graph can be created that shows the percentage of mastery on the first assessment followed by the second assessment and so on. The scores could then be recorded into chart form so that the results can be compared. Another way to chart the data might be an anecdotal record in which the strengths and weaknesses of the students are written in detail. Again, there is no one right way to do this; this is completely up to the individual teacher.

Reacting to data to change instruction does not have to be a complex and involved process. Let us review the seven steps of the Instructional Change process:

**Step 1:** Determine the area of instructional change.

**Step 2:** Determine ways to instruct the area that are different than the original mode of instruction.

**Tip:** When you begin using groups within your classroom remember to talk to your students first. This should occur at any level. Explain to the students that the groups are flexible and are based on data. Whenever possible, extend this information to parents as well. This will help everyone to understand that the grouping is a specific instructional choice and one that can and will change.

**Tip:** Each time you differentiate a unit, keep a folder for each of your flexible groups. In the folder include detailed lesson plans and anything else you need to plan for instruction. This will help you to build up differentiated or tiered lesson plans over time for each unit you teach.

**Step 3:** Determine the groups for instruction.

**Step 4:** Determine what instructional strategies will be used for each group, including details of what, how, where, and when.

**Step 5:** Determine how you will assess the learning.

**Step 6:** Determine what you will do in reaction to the information from the assessment.

**Step 7:** Determine how you will display the data if the instructional changes were effective.[/ul]

*A Plan for Instructional Change*, a tool to help work through the Instructional Change process, has been provided on page 85 in the Blueprints section of this book.

## A Final Word on Deciding How to Do It

In education, we become very adept at knowing what needs to be done; we sometimes lack the knowledge of how to do what needs to be done. One way to clearly determine that is by using a process called the Seven Steps for Instructional Change. In this process a teacher defines what needs to be done, different ways to do it, the different groups involved, specific strategies for implementation, assessment of instruction, further instructional changes and compilation of the data. This process is meant to "un-muddy" the waters as we navigate the world of data. Keep in mind that no cookie cutter answer exists; every student is different, every class is different, and every teacher is different. That's what makes teaching such a challenging and yet rewarding vocation. Things are never the same, and they are seldom what they seem. It takes in-depth analysis and a clear instructional plan to ensure success for all students—which is the final goal.

CHAPTER 5

# Specific Strategies for Specific Subjects

*We are continually faced with a series of great opportunities*
*brilliantly disguised as insoluble problems.*
— John W. Gardner

## Using the Instructional Change Process in the Main Content Areas

An instructional process such as differentiated instruction or the Instructional Change process is exactly just that—a process. Many times in education we are provided with the knowledge of a process, we learn the steps of a process, and we can even teach the process to someone else. What we can't always do is use the process. This is true with many instructional processes including backwards design, using formative assessment, and even the brain-based instructional strategies so prevalent today. We learn what they are, but unless the examples used are common to our own classroom situation, we are left to fill in the blanks. This chapter is going to address this. When asking teachers to use data to drive their instruction, what we are asking them to do is come up with different instruction for different students based on what they determine the students know or don't know. To really provide a "make and take it" as far as going beyond the data in analysis and instruction would mean taking every single possible example of data and spelling out in detail what should be done accordingly. That is actually already done in many textbooks where teachers are instructed what to do to reteach and extend knowledge. And to do this would mean writing a book of several thousand pages. Another point to consider is that at times students miss questions as a result of something extraneous. The reason for missing a question on an assessment may be due to the inability to answer higher level questions, confusion with specific questions due to wording or format, lack of prior knowledge, or any one of a dozen other reasons. How to teach higher level critical thinking skills and how to teach test-taking skills will be addressed in the next two chapters. Information will be provided here for each of the main core content areas, and while it is impossible to provide an example for every single situation, suggestions will be provided that can be adapted to all content and grade levels. When put into the Instructional Change process, these strategies will become the "how" of the process.

## Reading

When looking at the data in reading, most of the time deficits go back to one component of the reading process: reading comprehension. For whatever the reason, students are not able to answer a given question because they don't understand the information that was provided to them in the reading. This is one reason why the push is so strong to teach reading in all the different content areas at all grade levels. All teachers should be reading teachers. Given that, teaching students specific strategies to use when trying to understand the written text is critical. There are whole books written on this process and it is suggested that if the data points you to a weakness in reading comprehension skills, then further learning is recommended in the form of books, training sessions, and conferences. With that being said, there are some simple strategies that are easy to implement and use with students to improve reading comprehension. Research tells us that when students can make connections between their own lives and what is happening in the story, then reading comprehension increases. Here are several easy ways to move students to make connections as they read text:

- Provide students with a pad of "sticky" notes. Then every time they come across something in their reading that they can relate to themselves, or someone they know, have them write a couple of sentences about it on the sticky note, and place the note in the margins. You can even have three different colors of sticky notes for self, world, and text-to-text.

- Have students keep a "Connections Journal" in which they record any connection they have. These may include text-to-self connections, text-to-text connections, or text-to-world connections.

- Have students make "connection notations" in the margins of books as the connections are made. Students can code the connections T-S (text-to-self), T-T (text-to-text) or T-W (text-to-world).

- Have students fill out a *Connections Chart*. A blank one is provided for you on page 87 in the Blueprints section.

♦ Have students highlight connections. They can use different colored highlighters for the different types of connections.

In addition to making connections, there are several other simple strategies that can be used with students to increase their reading comprehension skills. Some of those strategies are described below.

♦ Have students write questions in the margins as questions come up. Then, exchange books with a friend who is reading the same book and have them answer the questions. Teachers can also review the questions to see what kinds of information students do not comprehend.

♦ Have students process visual information. They can do this through drawing pictures, or simply by having conversations about what they see in response to the text.

♦ Have students read in chunks. Have them read one or two paragraphs, then respond to what they read by answering a question, either verbally or orally.

The most important thing to remember when working with students on reading comprehension skills is to teach them the strategies, or what to do, when they do not understand something. Teaching students the strategies for comprehension is analogous to teaching someone to fish—you're giving them the power to control their own destiny.

## Writing

Written expression is a difficult skill for many students. When analyzing data from written assessments, it is sometimes hard to know if the problem is with the content, or if the student simply cannot communicate in written form. If the problem is with the content, that is an easy fix. If the problem, however, is the student's inability to communicate in writing, then that will impact the data in all subject areas—not just writing. Of course, this is assuming that the data analyzed is from an assessment on which students have to express their knowledge in writing. So, in tying instruction to the data in writing, it is important to analyze the reason why the student can't communicate. In some cases this may be because the student lacks the fine motor skills necessary to pen the words. If this is the case, then work on strengthening those muscles must be done and this, again, is an easy fix. If the problem lies in the area of expressive language, however, that is a very different story. A true language deficit may be considered a learning disability, and the student may need to be referred for testing in order to qualify for a specific program such as speech and language therapy. If the problem is not severe enough to warrant a special program, there are several strategies regular classroom teachers can use to strengthen skills in the area of writing.

The most important thing to remember when analyzing the data for instructional changes in writing, is to provide plenty of practice. One way of

**Tip:** For students with learning challenges many of these strategies may have to be done by reading the material to the student and then modeling how to use the strategies.

**Tip:** For gifted students you may want to add complexity to the process by not only providing the strategies, but then including some thought-provoking questions such as "What would it mean if…?" or "How might it change the plot of the story if…."

**Tip:** When using DiGIMS, or any other differentiated instructional software, make sure that you provide the Intervention teachers with the individualized student reports. This will not only aid them in the writing of the IEP, but also provide a connection between what the classroom teacher is doing and what the Intervention teacher is doing.

**Tip:** When working with students with learning challenges, the teacher may have to scribe for the student. This strategy will allow those students to express their thoughts without the roadblocks of writing. The student's writing can then be used to work on comprehension strategies.

**Tip:** When providing practice for gifted students in the area of writing, again, choice will give you the biggest bang for your buck. Gifted students often feel constrained by the regular curriculum; providing them the opportunity to explore topics of interest will lead to increased buy-in from them.

doing this is to schedule a daily writing time with minilessons taught at the beginning of each session. The minilessons should of course be specific to the data. The writing time itself should consist of both free writing (the student's choice) and assigned writing (the teacher's choice). Then, as the students work, the teachers can confer individually with students on their areas of weakness. Differentiation can also occur more easily within the daily writing time. Students could be asked to write on different subjects, or work on specific skills according to their needs. There are some computer programs that will allow writing teachers to input data on their students, then receive specific differentiated assignments for each student. One such program is DiGIMS, developed by Kim Hartman, a high school English teacher. When the process of grading essays and delivering differentiated assignments becomes too cumbersome and labor-heavy, DiGIMS provides a user-friendly way to track student progress in writing while providing individualized assignments to students according to need. See http://www.digimsonline.com.

One of the benefits of daily writing time is that students will begin to enjoy writing, especially if they have a choice. Allowing students to proceed at their own pace through the writing process—rough draft, revise and edit, publish—will help to make students more comfortable with expressing their thoughts in writing. Practice and individual daily intervention will allow students to improve their skills in writing, thereby leading to increased achievement in all academic content areas.

## Math

When analyzing the data in order to make instructional changes in math, perhaps the most significant deficit appears in the area of problem solving. What we often hear about, however, is the deficit in such low-level thinking skills as memorization of basic facts or formulas. To remediate the problem of memorization of basic facts, two things need to happen. First of all, more practice time must be given. Teachers often feel that they don't have the time to allow students to practice due to the enormity of the content they have to teach. A realistic view of this problem will show, however, that if the time isn't taken, then the problem may never be solved, thereby impacting any future success in the area of math. Second, students must do something different with regard to memorizing basic facts or formulas. Many times we simply have students do more of the same. If students can't learn the basic facts using a "drill and kill" method, then something different needs to be done. This might be accomplished through music, art, or physical activities. Brainstorming with other teachers having the same problems, and then planning different remediation activities and implementing them while partnering with those same teachers may be the answer. The bottom line is, if basic memorization of facts and formulas is hindering your student's progress and achievement, then you're going to need to devote the time and effort to change that.

Problem-solving skills may actually be the bigger obstacle when attempting to change instruction based on the data in math. Problem-solving skills require a systematic approach. They need to be taught deliberately to students, and there should be a consistent approach that's used. Vertically, teachers should discuss how much time they'll devote to teaching problem-solving strategies, how they'll teach them, and how they'll assess the learning of them. This should include all of the teachers in the system that teach math.

There are several very effective ways to teach problem solving. One way is the UPSC Method. This method has four steps:

**U**nderstand: think about what you're being asked to do. Make sure you understand the task.

**P**lan: plan your strategy for solving the problem.

**S**olve: work the problem using the strategy you chose.

**C**heck: work the problem one more time to make sure you have the correct answer.

Another formula for problem solving is the **THINK** method. In this method the student progresses through these five steps:

**T**alk about the problem.

**H**ow can the problem be solved?

**I**dentify a strategy for solving the problem.

**N**otice how the strategy helped you solve the problem.

**K**eep thinking about the problem.

As in reading, math strategies should be intentionally and purposefully taught to students. Students should understand that they have many different strategies in their repertoire from which to choose to solve problems. Some of these strategies are

- draw pictures whenever you can
- use or make a table
- make an organized list
- guess and check
- make it simpler
- work backwards
- use or look for a pattern
- act out or use manipulatives
- use logical reasoning
- brainstorm

**Tip:** When working with students with learning challenges try to teach a process for problem solving that has only a couple of steps. For example, the steps might be as simple as #1-What is the problem asking you to do? And #2-How will you do it?

**Tip:** When working with gifted students try to always go one question beyond the standard process. For example, ask a question like "If you could make up another way to solve the same problem, what would it be?"

One of the most important strategies to teach students in math is to always ask themselves the question, "Does this make sense?" This question should be posted in the classroom, asked aloud during class, and even used as a question on an assessment.

One way to make sure students are using strategies in math is to have them record and keep track of the strategies they use. This can be done through a strategy notebook. In a strategy notebook, the student is asked to list the strategy used on a chart. This chart can be used to track which strategies students use the most often. You can also use this information to make classroom tally charts, to graph favorite strategies, or even to evaluate the different strategies. A couple of different strategy record-keeping forms, *Problem Solving Strategy Record Keeper* and *Problem Solving Journal*, are included on pages 88 and 89 in the Blueprints section.

## Social Studies

When examining the data in the subject of social studies, it is sometimes difficult to pinpoint exactly where the problems lie. Social studies is a subject in which the teaching strategies have changed dramatically. With the advent of the Internet, it is apparent that students today can no longer memorize every important date or event in history. The world is changing at an incredible rate. We can no longer try to fill students' minds with facts. We need to teach concepts. Specifically, we need to teach students how to analyze situations and find answers to problems. The role of the teacher in the social studies classroom has shifted to become one of a facilitator of learning. To that end, when going beyond the data in social studies, we should look at teaching students how to analyze situations, charts, graphs, and data.

In order to analyze information in charts, graphs, and diagrams, it is necessary for students to be able to interpret information in these forms. To that end, there are some specific strategies that teachers can use to teach students these skills. Most of the time we give students information in these formats and then ask them to answer questions about the information without really teaching them how to draw out the information. One way to ensure that your students know how to interpret information in graphic organizers is to have them identify points of content in these charts, graphs, and diagrams. Try giving them a chart or diagram, and then ask a questions such as

> "What information would you expect to find in the first square of this flowchart?"

or

> "Highlight the main points made in this informational web."

In this way students are looking at the graphic organizer as something that will provide them information to eventually answer questions. They are, in essence, practicing how to interpret graphic organizers.

Another way to teach students to interpret information in graphic organizers is to give them some information and have them compile it into a graph, chart, or diagram. Then, have the students themselves come up with questions that can be answered by studying the graphic organizer. Through this backwards-building approach, students will learn the true use and application of graphic organizers. That's when you can move on and teach the student to analyze the information found in these visual formats.

Analysis is a higher level thinking skill. Analysis means to look closely at something, virtually taking it apart and finding relationships and generalities among the different components. Most of us were never taught how to analyze something. One easy strategy to use when teaching students to analyze something is have them look at the similarities and differences. This can be done in every situation. Take for example, the two world wars. How were they alike? How were they different? This might start out as two simple charts in which the main components or facts of each war are listed. Then, the similarities can be explored. What things were the same? These can be written either on a separate chart or on a graphic organizer. Another way to pull out the similarities and differences is to give the students summaries of the facts of both wars and have them highlight the similarities in one color and the differences in a another color. Once students begin to become accustomed to finding similarities and differences, you can lead them into other areas of higher level thinking. For example, they could evaluate which of the wars they felt had a stronger impact on our economy. Or, they can synthesize by describing how changing a component of one of the wars might have changed the outcome. By teaching students to analyze, they'll be able to more effectively take apart information that they are given—an important learning skill.

Once students have learned to read and analyze graphic organizers, they can then learn to use graphic organizers for their own informational analysis. Students should know and understand that an easy way to compile information is to place that information into some type of a visual organizer. Using graphic organizers means completing graphic organizers to better understand something. Specific graphic organizers that could be used include similarities and differences charts, flowcharts, timelines, main idea webs or even a KWL (What Do I Know? What Do I Want to Know? What Did I Learn?) chart. Several of these graphic organizers are included in the Blueprints section. See *Venn Diagram* (90), *Comparison Matrix* (91), *T-Chart* (92), *Category Chart* (93), and *Circle Category Chart* (94).

**Tip:** When working with students with learning challenges keep the graphic organizer, chart, or graph simple. Have the students do one thing at a time; for example, have them find similarities between things. Later, you can add the aspect of differences.

**Tip:** When working with gifted students think about having them make up their own graphic organizer to analyze a situation. Or, have them develop a graphic organizer for the rest of the class.

## Science

When intentionally changing instruction based on the data in science one thing to look at is how well students understand cause and effect. Cause and effect is the main premise behind scientific concepts. Studying cause

**■ Figure 5.1** Cause and Effect T-Chart for Older Students

| Cause | Effect |
|---|---|
| ♦ A terrorist attempted to ignite an explosive device in an airplane. | ♦ Stricter precautions are taken at airport security stations. |
| ♦ Many people were dying from the flu. | ♦ A vaccination was developed. |
| ♦ A tornado warning was in effect. | ♦ The people took cover in the basement. |

**■ Figure 5.2** What-So T-Chart for Younger Students

| What | So |
|---|---|
| ♦ It rained. | ♦ I got wet. |
| ♦ It is hot. | ♦ I started to sweat. |
| ♦ I love ice cream. | ♦ I ate ice cream for dessert. |

and effect is what scientists do. Therefore, students need to understand that for every cause there is an effect. This needs to be instructed in a clear, intentional manner. We cannot assume that students automatically know this. We need to teach students strategies to use when analyzing cause and effect. One such strategy is to make a cause and effect chart. This can be in the format of a T-chart. The words at the top should be grade appropriate. For younger students, you would want to write the words, "What" and "So," while for older students you could use the words "Cause" and "Effect." Then, write events in the first column, and brainstorm the effects in the second column. An example of each of these charts is shown in Figures 5.1 and 5.2. In addition, blank *Cause and Effect* and *What-So* charts can be found on pages 95 and 96 in the Blueprints section.

Another way to teach cause and effect is to play "If . . . Then." This is a game that could be written down or played aloud. Simply put, two people play this game. The first person gives a scenario, and the second person responds back with what would logically happen as a result of the "If." For example:

**Tip:** When working with learning challenged students, start with very obvious cause and effect relationships and then work up to more difficult ones.

| **Student 1** | **Student 2** |
|---|---|
| "**If** I had no money | . . . **Then** I couldn't buy a new bike." |

One final strategy to use when teaching students cause and effect is to have them work backwards. This is accomplished by giving the student the effect first, then have them provide the cause. For example, if the effect is

"I turned on the light."

then the cause might be

"It was dark outside."

This type of exercise could be done orally, or in written form. It could be done as a game, or as a practice task. The important thing to remember when teaching students cause and effect is that you will need to model for the students and allow them a lot of practice time. Understanding cause and effect will help students increase their skills in not only science, but all of the core content areas.

## A Final Word on Specific Strategies for Specific Subjects

When looking at the data in order to make intentional instructional changes in specific subjects, there are several things that can be done to get the best results for your efforts. In reading, working on reading comprehension skills and strategies will lead to changes in the data, while in math working on problem-solving strategies will have a positive effect on the data. Analyzing information in visual organizers in social studies will help students perform better on subsequent assessments. In science, being able to determine and understand cause and effect will lead to increased understanding in this subject. Any and all of these skills, it should be noted, are cross-curricular; that is, if students increase their aptitude in these skills, they are almost certain to increase achievement in all academic areas.

A sure strategy to use when changing instruction based on the data in any subject is to provide differentiated instruction immediately. Forming short-term flexible groups to work on areas of deficit as well as areas of extension are imperative if the results of the data are going to be affected. Collaborating with other colleagues to develop and implement lesson plans can be an effective way to do this. The important thing to remember is to respond to the data immediately and to have goals in mind that will allow you to do what is best for your students and their future achievement.

**Tip:** When working with gifted students have them add on effects to the cause. For example, if the cause is "It is raining," then the effect would be "I got wet." Next, take that a step further. "I got wet" is the cause so "I dripped water on the floor" is the effect. Then, "I dripped water on the floor" is the cause, so "The floor became slippery" is the effect and so on and so on. This could easily be made into a graphic organizer or a flowchart, for example.

# CHAPTER 6

# Specific Strategies to Increase Critical Thinking Skills

*The real process of education should be the process of learning to think through the application of real problems.*
—John Dewey

## Moving Our Students to Higher Level Thinking Skills

One of the instructional implications that we educators often derive from our data is that our students need to become better at higher level, critical thinking skills. We've studied our state tests, our unit tests, and even our daily assignments and quizzes and found that the higher level questions are the ones with which students have the most trouble. So we know that we need to become better at teaching higher level, critical thinking skills. Now comes the big problem—how do we do this? Most of us are familiar with Bloom's Taxonomy; we dutifully memorized the different levels in our undergraduate classes. But, how many of us actually learned how to teach students to use higher level, critical thinking skills? This chapter will provide simple, easy-to-use strategies for pushing your students up into those higher levels of thinking. But first, a brief definition of the different levels of Bloom's Taxonomy.

# Basic Bloom's

The first level of Bloom's Taxonomy is Knowledge. (This level is named "Understanding" in the Revised Bloom's Taxonomy.) It is at this level that students are asked to recall basic literal information. This is what students do when we ask them what something is, or we ask them to list something. Knowledge is considered to be the lowest of Bloom's levels. Unfortunately, this is the level at which many students are instructed a vast majority of the time. An example of a knowledge-level question is shown below.

**What is the setting in the story *Goldilocks and the Three Bears?***

The second level of Bloom's Taxonomy is Comprehension or Understanding. This is where we asked students to demonstrate understanding of something. When students are asked to explain something, they're operating at the Comprehension level of Bloom's. This is the level that many teachers take students to when they are trying to raise the rigor in the classroom. Unfortunately, this is sometimes as far as they go. An example of a comprehension-level question is shown below.

**Explain the difference between a fact and an opinion.**

Application, or Using, is the third level of Bloom's. Students are applying information when they're asked to use something they've learned in a new situation. The key to this description is using something that they've already learned. Students are asked to do this more often in certain subjects. Take for example, math. Students are taught a math formula, and then asked to use that formula to solve new problems. In art, students are taught the skill of shading, and then asked to demonstrate this skill in a new drawing. Below is an application question.

**Rewrite the following sentence using contractions wherever you can:**

**I will not cry because I did not get invited to the party.**

It is important to note at this time that the first three levels of Bloom's Taxonomy—Knowledge, Comprehension, and Application—are all considered to be lower level thinking levels. That's because you're taking information that has already been learned and doing nothing different or new with it. It just is what it is. That's not to say that thinking at these levels is easy; try memorizing all of the world capitals and you'll find this is a difficult task. But when thinking at these levels, you're not being asked to go beyond what is; in other words you're not being asked to do anything extraneous with the knowledge.

The next level of Bloom's Taxonomy is Analysis or Analyzing. When we ask students to operate at this level of thinking we're definitely asking them to employ higher level, critical thinking skills. It's in this level that we ask students to make generalizations and find evidence to support those generalizations. This is when we ask students to scrutinize something and find relationships between things. Here's an example of an analysis-level question:

**How did the assassination of Dr. Martin Luther King change the political nature of the United States at the time?**

The next higher thinking level of Bloom's Taxonomy is Synthesis, or Creating. When students are asked to think at the Synthesis level, they are being asked to take apart something that they have learned and make something new with it. This is what happens when we asked students to write a different ending to a story, or think of a different way to solve a math problem. Here's an example of a Synthesis level question.

**Change one of the variables in the scientific experiment in your book, and describe how that will change the outcome of the experiment.**

The last level of Bloom's Taxonomy, Evaluation or Evaluating, is also considered to be higher level. When we ask students to evaluate something, we're asking them to judge something according to a set criteria, and then justify the judgment. This is what students do when we ask them to tell us the easiest way to do something, or we ask them which character they like best and why. Here's an example of an evaluation-level question.

**Which world event do you think most influenced the women's rights movement and why—the right to vote, or Title IV? Justify your choice.**

It's imperative that you understand the different levels of Bloom's Taxonomy, especially those considered to be the higher level, critical thinking ones, if you're going to move your students up to those higher levels of thinking.

**Tip:** Higher level, critical thinking skills are not developmental. Eighteen- month-old children use higher level thinking as they acquire language; they constantly analyze, synthesize, and evaluate information. Sometimes knowing that very young children use critical thinking skills can help as we try to move older students into these levels of thinking.

**Tip:** Understand that each level of Bloom's Taxonomy builds on the next level. In other words, you cannot synthesize something unless you can analyze it, apply it, understand it, and know it.

## Up to Analysis

Even if you're not an expert in critical thinking, or the levels of Bloom's Taxonomy, there are still easy ways to teach your students higher level thinking skills when the data dictates it. Teaching students to analyze means that they need to be taught to break apart information and examine the parts.

One easy way to bump students up to analysis is to ask them to compare and contrast. This can be done

**In reading...**

How are the two characters in the book *Bridge to Terabithia* alike? How are they different?

**In writing...**

Describe how a persuasive piece of writing and an editorial in a newspaper are alike. How are they different?

**In math...**

Study the two shapes in Figure 6.1.

■ **Figure 6.1**   Shapes

Fill out the Similarities and Differences Chart in Figure 6.2 to show how they are alike and how they are different.

■ **Figure 6.2**   Similarities and Differences Chart

| Similarities | Differences |
|---|---|
|  |  |

**In social studies...**

Write two paragraphs, one describing how the Korean War and the Vietnam War were alike and one describing how they were different. Include cultural, economic, environmental, and psychological comparisons.

*I Have the Data...Now What?*

**Or in science...**

Complete the Venn Diagram in Figure 6.3 comparing and contrasting two natural disasters. Choose from an earthquake, a tornado, a tsunami, a hurricane, or a flood.

■ **Figure 6.3**   Venn Diagram

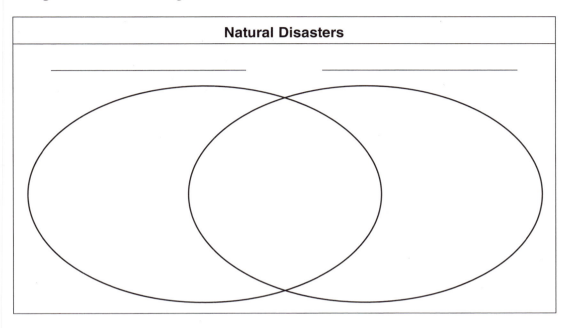

In addition to having students find similarities and differences, there are many other easy strategies to move students up into the analysis level of thinking. The chart in Figure 6.4 lists some of these strategies.

■ **Figure 6.4**   Easy Ways to Teach Analysis

**Easy Ways to Teach Analysis**

♦ Have students classify things into groups and then explain the reasons for the classification.

♦ Ask students to look at several possible correct answers and determine which answer is the best answer.

♦ Ask students to tell you which answer is not a correct answer and why. This can be done in all subject areas.

♦ Have students complete analogies: _____ is to _____ as _____ is to _____.

♦ Have students make hypotheses before learning something. Then, have them compare the actual answer/outcome with the hypotheses.

♦ Have students find the cause and effect for different situations.

Another easy way to get students to analyze is to ask them a series of questions. These questions are provided in the *Analysis Chart* on page 97 in the Blueprints section.

## Up to Synthesis

When teaching students to synthesize information, we're asking them to take information they already know and put it together in a different way. A simple way to push students into the synthesis level of thinking is to show them one scenario and ask them to think of a different scenario.

This can be done

### In reading...

At the end of the book *Goldilocks and the Three Bears.* Goldilocks ran away after the bears found her in Baby Bear's bed. Tell how the plot of the story would have to change in order to change the ending.

### In writing...

One way to persuade someone to do something is to write them a letter. Read the following letter and rewrite it as an editorial in the newspaper. Remember, you are trying to persuade the reader.

> Dear Students,
>
> We need to take action immediately! The administration is trying to take away our right to leave the school campus at lunch. This is not fair for several reasons. First of all, the number of students who abuse this privilege is a very small percentage of the student population. Secondly, the cafeteria would be so crowded if everyone were forced to stay on campus that many students would not have time to eat because it would take too long to go through the line. Lastly, for many of us getting away from campus gives us a well-needed break so that we are ready to learn in the afternoon.
>
> If you feel as we do about this injustice, please join us in protesting by meeting in the office at 3:00 this afternoon.
>
> The Poly Sci Club

### In math...

The students in Mrs. Johnson's class were given the following problem to solve:

**Tip:** It's easy to get comprehension and analysis confused. When you are trying to ascertain whether you are requiring your students to demonstrate understanding or demonstrate analysis, focus on the relationship part of analysis. Are the students really breaking the information apart and examining the information to determine relationships between concepts, or are they simply showing you they understand a concept?

$286 + 365 =$ _____.

Juan solved the problem the following way:

```
  2 2 1
+ 3 6 5
-------
  5 8 6
```

Show a different way to solve the same problem. Do your work in the space below.

**In social studies...**

The Civil War ended with the North on the winning side. This resulted in the end of slavery. Describe what our country might be like today if the South had won the Civil War. Include at least three things that would be different today.

**And in science...**

The use of computers has made our lives easier today in many different ways. Describe how life today would be different if computers had never been invented.

There are several different, easy ways to move students up into the Synthesis Level of critical thinking. These different strategies are listed in the chart in Figure 6.5.

In addition, there are several simple steps that you can have students go through to move them to synthesis. The *Synthesis Chart* is provided for this purpose on page 98 in the Blueprints section.

**Tip:** An easy way to think of the process of synthesis is by thinking of it as baking a cake. You take all of the ingredients and put them together to make something new...a cake!

■ **Figure 6.5**   Easy Ways to Teach Synthesis

---

**Easy Ways to Teach Synthesis**

♦ Predict what is going to happen in situations before they occur.

♦ List factors that may make something better or worse.

♦ Play "What if...?"

♦ Think up an invention to solve a problem.

♦ Have students tell how a story would be different if some element of the story were to change. Ex.: the main character might be a boy instead of a girl, the setting might change, etc.

---

# Up to Evaluation

The Evaluation level of Bloom's taxonomy is more than just giving an opinion. This level requires students to form judgments and defend them based on a set of criteria. The important part of this level is the criteria part that provides the parameters for this level of thinking. An easy way to provide students with the opportunity to evaluate information is to give them two answers to a problem and ask them which they think is the best answer and why. Evaluating might look like this

### In reading...

Suppose the Three Bears caught Goldilocks after she ran out of their house. They could either have her arrested, or take her home to her parent's house and let them punish her. Which way do you think would be the best way to handle the situation that would be the fairest for all involved? Make sure you justify your choice.

### In writing...

Suppose you were trying to persuade someone to do something that you wanted them to do. You have the option of writing them a letter, texting them, or writing them an e-mail. Which way do you think would be the best way to handle this so that you have the optimum chance of getting your way? Defend your choice.

### In math...

The students in Mrs. Murdock's class were given the following problem to solve:

$$3\,6\,5 + 4\,2\,2 = \underline{\hspace{1cm}}.$$

Heather solved the problem this way:

| 3 0 0 | | 6 0 | | 5 | | |
|-------|---|-----|---|---|---|---|
| + 4 0 0 | | + 2 0 | | + 2 | | |
| 7 0 0 | + | 8 0 | + | 7 | = | 787 |

John solved the problem this way:

```
  3 6 5
+ 4 2 2
  7 8 7
```

Which way do you think is the easiest way to solve the problem? Justify your choice.

*I Have the Data... Now What?*

**In social studies...**

Imagine that you are developing a brand new country and you have to decide the type of government to rule your country. Democracy is not one of your options. You have to decide between a socialist government or a monarchy. Choose which government you would choose to run your country. Justify your choice.

**And finally in science...**

People have very strong feelings toward stem-cell research. Choose a side and explain in detail why you support the side you choose.

As with the levels of Analysis and Synthesis, there are several simple things you can ask students to do to move them up to the evaluation level of thinking. Some of these strategies are listed in the Figure 6.6.

As in the other two levels, the Evaluation level of thinking may be reached by answering just a few simple questions. The tool for this, *Evaluation Chart*, is on page 99 in the Blueprints section.

**Tip:** One of the most important parts of evaluation is the justification of the answer. Teach your students to always justify their opinions. This may mean teaching them the criteria for a justification. For example, "because I like it" is not an acceptable justification; you must give two reasons in your justification, etc.

■ **Figure 6.6** Easy Ways to Teach Evaluation

**Easy Ways to Teach Evaluation**

♦ Have students tell their favorite of something and why they feel that way.

♦ Have students take a side on something and argue the point.

♦ Give students an answer and have them tell you if they think it is the best answer and why.

♦ Have students tell which school rule they would like to change and why.

♦ Give students a couple of different scenarios for ending of books and ask them which one they prefer and why.

♦ Have students debate political issues.

♦ Have students create rules for the classroom.

# A Final Word on Specific Strategies to Increase Critical Thinking Skills

Though the data may determine that our students need to increase their skills in thinking at the higher, critical thinking levels, the way to accomplish this is often unclear. Many of us are not skilled ourselves in critical thinking, and when assessing our activities in our own classrooms, we find that we are mostly operating within the lower levels of Bloom's Taxonomy. There are some easy steps and strategies that can be taken to move students into the higher, critical levels of thinking. Asking students to make comparisons, make hypotheses, tell how to do something in a different way, and tell which of two things is the better choice are easy ways to move students up into the higher, critical levels of thinking. The best way to help students become critical thinkers, however, is to become better critical thinkers ourselves. This may entail reading more about critical thinking skills, taking classes on critical thinking, going to workshops and trainings on critical thinking, and most important, providing a lot of practice in critical thinking activities. This is the surest way to ensure that we can respond to the data when the data tells us that our students need to increase their critical thinking skills.

# CHAPTER 7

# Specific Strategies to Increase Test-Taking Skills

*I didn't fail the test. I just found 100 ways to do it wrong.*
—Benjamin Franklin

## Why Teach Test-Taking Skills?

In this world of high-stakes testing, one thing has become abundantly clear: we need to teach students how to take tests—like it or not. This becomes even more important as we analyze data and struggle to figure out a) if the student has not learned what was taught, or b) if it was the test that created the difficulty. This leads to several very important questions. First of all, how do we teach students how to take a test? Then, who's responsible for teaching them? Finally, how will we know that they've learned test-taking skills—the assessment of the assessment if you will? This chapter will answer those very important questions. Also, this chapter will provide very specific, easy-to-use strategies for students to employ as they navigate through the world of high-stakes tests.

The most obvious answer to this question is that test-taking skills should be taught to ensure that the test format or vocabulary isn't getting in the way of the students' demonstrating mastery of learning. With that being said, it can be argued that even those students who score very well on assessments can benefit from basic test-taking skills as they continue their higher education and perhaps more rigorous testing. One thing we know is that almost every vocation, and even basic life situations, requires the ability to take tests.

It would be common sense, then, to teach these skills continually and consistently, beginning at a very early age. Yet, we don't see this happen in an organized manner in most schools. Some teachers are very adept at teaching test-taking skills, while others aren't. So for the student, it is, in essence, the luck of the draw. You could be a middle school student in Mrs. Simpson's class and receive some quality instruction on how to take tests, or you could be in Mr. Riley's class and receive no instruction whatsoever on how to manage a test. That leads to a lot of inequity where these skills are concerned. For that reason alone, we all should be more specific and succinct when instructing test-taking skills.

## The Link Between Test-Taking Skills and the Standards

Many educators feel that they already have too much to do—too many standards to teach, too many students to teach, too many fiscal and environmental obstacles to overcome. That's why specifically teaching test-taking skills often falls very far down the priority list. Again, if you're truly trying to change instruction based on data, the first thing you need to do is ascertain if the students are failing to show mastery on an assessment because they truly didn't learn, or because they don't understand the skill of test taking.

If the inability of students to take a test is interfering with their demonstrating mastery, then that variable needs to be eliminated. The good news is teaching test-taking skills falls right in line with the standards. In reading, all students need to learn how to comprehend what it is they're reading. Likewise, all students need to learn how to follow directions. The skill of reading and interpreting graphs and charts shows up not just in reading, but in the subjects of math, social studies and even science.

So what is the most effective step to take if you are trying to find the time to include test-taking skills into the curriculum? Figure out which of the standards can be taught through the instruction of test-taking skills. Once that is done, you can remove those standards (or the direct instruction of those standards) from another subject area, thus freeing up some of the time in which other things can be taught. The first step in this process is to look at the standards that you teach, and tag those that fall into the category of test-taking skills. Another way to look at this is to think about which of the standards would be specifically helpful to a student taking a test. An example of this can be found in Figure 7.1. which details grade-four academic content standards.

The items in the second column of this chart are the test-taking skills that align with the standards. What this means is that if those skills were intentionally taught to students, then they would strengthen, or perhaps even take

**Tip:** Don't think of it as "teaching to the test" but rather think of it as "teaching the students the skills necessary to be successful on the test."

*I Have the Data... Now What?*

**■ Figure 7.1**   Standard and Test-Taking Alignment Chart

| Subject Area/Standard | Test-Taking Skills |
|---|---|
| **English Language Arts:** | |
| ♦ Define the meaning of unknown words by using context clues. | ♦ Use context clues. |
| ♦ Select, create and use graphic organizers to interpret textual information. | ♦ Interpret information in charts, graphs, and diagrams. |
| ♦ Demonstrate comprehension of grade-appropriate material. | ♦ Use comprehension strategies to understand what is read. |
| ♦ Analyze information found in maps, charts, tables, graphs, and diagrams. | ♦ Interpret information in charts, graphs, and diagrams. |
| **Math:** | |
| ♦ Justify a general rule for a pattern by using visual representation, tables or graphs. | ♦ Interpret information in charts, graphs, and diagrams. |
| ♦ Model problems with visual representations and use graphs and tables to draw conclusions and make predictions. | ♦ Interpret information in charts, graphs, and diagrams. |
| ♦ Read and interpret complex displays of data such as double bar graphs, frequency tables, and circle graphs. | ♦ Interpret information in charts, graphs, and diagrams. |
| **Social Studies:** | |
| ♦ Understand, interpret, and use maps to aid comprehension. | ♦ Interpret information in charts, graphs, and diagrams. |
| ♦ Analyze the reliability of facts within information. | ♦ Determine important information in text. |
| ♦ Draw inferences from relevant information. | ♦ Determine important information in text. |
| **Science:** | |
| ♦ Use evidence and observations to explain and communicate the results of investigations. | ♦ Summarize information. |
| ♦ Develop descriptions, explanations, and models using evidence to defend/support findings. | ♦ Summarize information. |

the place of, the standards on the left. Instruction time could be transferred to the test-taking time, or at least integrated into the subject area content. A blank *Standard and Test-Taking Alignment Chart* has been provided on page 100 in the Blueprints section.

# Teaching Test Taking as a Genre

Many reading teachers today are suggesting that one way to teach test-taking skills is to teach them as a separate genre. In much the same way that we teach students the genre of poetry or drama, or even nonfiction, tests all have certain characteristics and need to be approached in a very different way than, say, a fiction piece. Reading tests requires an understanding of the format of the test, as well as the vocabulary of the test. Also included in this is the ability to read and understand bulleted lists, and certainly charts and graphs. It makes sense, then, to treat the art of reading tests as a completely separate genre. If this was incorporated into the curriculum as a separate unit, it would solve the time problem. It could be instructed within the reading period and then integrated into the other subject areas.

In teaching test taking as a genre, teachers need to understand themselves the different skills needed for success. Specifically, teachers need to know the strategies that students should employ when reading and understanding tests. An easy way to determine this is to sit down with one of the tests your students will need to take, such as the state test, an end-of-the-course exam, and so on, and read through it as if you were the student. Then, list the different skills you need to be able to utilize to be successful on each item. For example, study Figure 7.2. and the question below, taken from the Ohio Achievement Assessment for Grade 5 Social Studies.

Looking at this question through the eyes of a fifth grader, you can see that the student needs to be able to do the following things:

♦ Read fluently at grade level
♦ Make inferences
♦ Interpret a graph
♦ Make comparisons
♦ Summarize information

In addition, the student needs to be able to navigate the format of the multiple-choice question, and know that the information in the box is important. If students don't see this information prior to taking the test, they may not be able to put all of the components necessary for success together. *Skills in the Genre of Test-Taking Chart*, a tool designed to help compile the components or the skills needed to be successful on any given test, is provided on page 101 in the Blueprints section.

# Specific Test-Taking Skills

There are many different strategies that students can be taught to help prepare them for the world of tests. These strategies are ones that the students

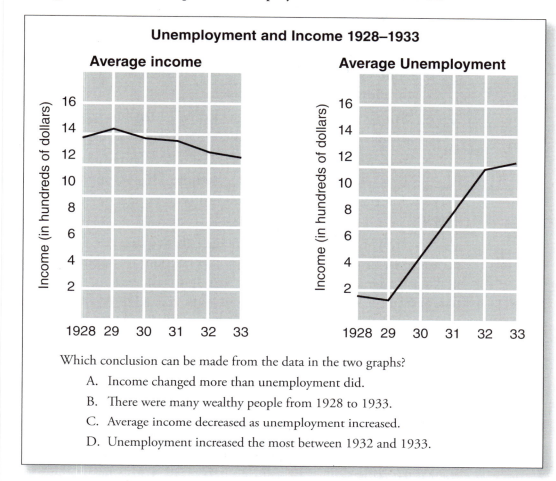

**■ Figure 7.2**   Two Graphs of Unemployment and Income Data

**Unemployment and Income 1928–1933**

**Average income**

**Average Unemployment**

Which conclusion can be made from the data in the two graphs?

A. Income changed more than unemployment did.

B. There were many wealthy people from 1928 to 1933.

C. Average income decreased as unemployment increased.

D. Unemployment increased the most between 1932 and 1933.

can use a) prior to, b) during, and c) after the test to increase achievement. If test taking is indeed taught as a genre, then teaching these skills in this order makes sense. For this purpose, then, the skills of test taking will be divided into these three categories.

## Prior to the Test

Several behaviors need to happen before the test begins as they have been proven to be extremely important in regard to test performance. These are often taken for granted, but in fact we need to be very intentional about teaching them to our students. Here are some of these prior behaviors:

◆ Get a good night's sleep prior to the test. This should be discussed with both the student and the parent.

◆ Eat a good breakfast prior to the test. Again, information about what constitutes a good breakfast should be discussed with both the student and the parent. If eating a good breakfast at home isn't a possibility, then a good breakfast should be provided at school.

- Learn how to relax prior to the test. This includes breathing exercises, visualization strategies, and stretching exercises. Teach these techniques prior to the test, and then practice them regularly.

- Use the restroom prior to the test. Don't drink a lot of liquids beforehand, especially if the testing environment isn't one in which students are allowed a restroom break.

- Work on time management skills. Learn how to break tasks down into several smaller tasks; then practice this skill.

- Work on test-stamina skills. This can be accomplished by taking smaller "tests" in a formal test-taking setting. This will build endurance—sort of like a marathon runner who runs 10 miles a day prior to the big race!

One useful tool when preparing students for a test is to have them fill out a contract. This contract should include things that the student is willing to do ahead of time to increase the chances of them feeling relaxed and ready. If necessary, a contract can also be drawn up for the parent, or even between the parent and the student. For your convenience, a blank *Test Prep Contract* has been provided for you on page 102 in the Blueprints section.

## During the Test

There are many different test-taking strategies that students can be taught to utilize during a test. Again, the important thing to remember is that these skills need to be both taught and practiced prior to the actual test. Below is a list of some of the things you might teach students to do to help them increase their test-taking skills. This is just a partial list; whole books have been written on this subject and it's recommended that you further research this topic if you plan to institute a test-taking curriculum into your school or classroom.

- Read the questions prior to any reading selection, chart, or graph that's included as a stimulus for the question. Then, go back and read the question a second time after reading the stimulus. Reading the question first will help direct your thinking.

- Always restate the question in your answer on the constructed-response questions. If the question asks, "What are the three branches of government?" the answer should begin, "The three branches of government are...." This strategy not only allows for the completion of a thought without interruption, but has been shown to dramatically increase comprehension skills, especially for struggling learners.

- Circle or underline any important words that you need to pay attention to in the question before you even attempt to answer it. Some examples of these key words are: *the best answer, two reasons, compare or contrast information, list, explain, analyze, solve, show your work*, etc. Carry this skill over into all classroom assignments.

- For struggling learners: if you're allowed to use a highlighter, highlight all of the words you know how to read before you begin. You will be amazed that you will know at least one half of the words before you begin. Use your context clues to figure out the rest.

- When checking back over your test, start at the end. That will give you a different look at your test than the one you had the first time.

- Always show your work, especially in math. If a grader can see your thinking, you may earn some points.

- Use graphic organizers to organize your thoughts. For example, if you are asked to write a retelling, jot down your ideas in a Beginning/Middle/Middle/End chart like the one in Figure 7.3.

■ **Figure 7.3** Beginning/Middle/Middle/End Chart

| B | M | M | E |
|---|---|---|---|
|   |   |   |   |

This can be done quickly in the margins of the test. You need to bullet your ideas, but this will serve to allow you to compose your thoughts before you start. You also won't fade out at the end; you will be able to finish strong.

- If you are stuck on a question, skip it. But don't forget to go back to it. If you're allowed to have those sticky tabs, use those to mark the section that you need to go back to. If you aren't allowed sticky tabs, keep a tally on the front of the test that you can erase at the end. A tally should be made for each question you skip. You can also write the question number if you need to be more specific.

- Read all the answer choices for the multiple choice questions before deciding on an answer. Remember, sometimes there is more than one "right" answer; the question may be asking for the "best" answer.

- Read all directions very carefully. Think about what the directions are telling you before you begin. If you're at all confused, ask for clarification.

A useful tool for the strategies that students can use during a test is a chart listing them. Have the students refer to the chart during any type of testing activity in class. If possible, use the list as a checklist while you're preparing for the test. If you're permitted, keep the list posted so that all students can view it during the test. (Remember to check your state's test rules to see if this is permissible.)

## After the Test

Having the students reflect on the experience following the test can serve as a valuable learning tool for future tests and serve to increase test-taking skills. The reflection can be as simple as a journal entry or as detailed as a questionnaire developed specifically for the test. The following questions are some that the students could be asked during the reflection process:

♦ What do you think went really well? What do you think could have gone better?

♦ With which type of questions did you have the most difficulty? Was it a specific format? (for example, multiple choice or constructed response?) Which type of question did you find to be the least difficult?

♦ Do you think the questions you missed were because of
  ◇ fatigue?
  ◇ not understanding the concept?
  ◇ not understanding what you were suppose to do?
  ◇ miscalculating?
  ◇ not reading everything?
  ◇ rushing through?

♦ If you could take this test again, what would you do differently?

♦ As a result of taking this test, what do you feel you still need help with?

♦ Did you feel prepared for this test? Why or why not?

Sometimes discussing these things together as a class and making a class list is enough. This may be more appropriate for students in the lower elementary grades. At other times it may be necessary to have individual, written reflections about the testing experience. Whatever the choice, the best way to increase test-taking skills is to make certain that a goal comes out of the reflections. The goal may be as small as "I will read all of the selection and the question before I attempt to answer the question," or as detailed as "I will memorize all of my multiplication facts before the next math test." Remember, a part of a goal is to determine the evidence that shows the goal has been met. For your convenience, three *Posttest-Reflection Sheets* have been included on pages 103–105 in the Blueprints section, including one you can use for very young students.

**Tip:** Having students reflect on their performance after a test may seem like a luxury time-wise, and one that you might think you cannot afford. Know that research shows that when students reflect and take ownership of their learning, achievement gains are made. This is worth spending time on!

*I Have the Data...Now What?*

## Specific Things Teachers Can Do

The main emphasis thus far has been on things the student should do with regard to test-taking skills. As with any type of instruction, there are specific things that the teacher can do to prepare the students for the testing experience. Some of these strategies are listed below.

- Give students a test with short answer questions and instead of having them answer the question, have them mark the different parts of the question that needs to be answered.
- Give the students a test and instead of having them take the test, have them go back to the text, chart, graph, etc., and highlight where they find the information they need to answer the question. They can place the question number next to the highlighted words.
- Give the students a test and instead of having them take the test, have them explain exactly what the question is asking them to do in their own words.

In addition, it is really important to discuss how the test-taking skills will be taught and this should be consistent within a school/district. For example, will the reading teacher teach these skills? Or will it be the media specialist, the intervention teacher, or the school counselor? Who will come up with the curriculum? How will these skills be supported in the other subject areas? What will be the assessment of learning for the test-taking skills? Will you have a written assessment, a performance assessment, or perhaps several centers in which students demonstrate good test-taking skills? How can you share these skills with the parent? These are all questions that will need to be answered if you are going to put a standardized test-taking class or curriculum into effect.

## A Final Word on Specific Strategies to Increase Test-Taking Skills

If teachers are really going to use data to change instruction, they need to be able to ascertain if the data is demonstrating a lack of content skills or a lack of test-taking skills. One way to do this is to build test-taking skills intentionally into your curriculum. In order to do that you need to be very purposeful in planning who will teach these skills, exactly what will be taught, and how you'll know the students have learned what has been taught. A good outline for a test-taking unit would be to provide instruction in strategies and skills that the student can use prior to the test, during the test, and following the test. Specific strategies have been provided that address each of these

**Tip:** Standardizing grading procedures in a school will help to increase student achievement. Research shows that when the interpretation of a rule is the same for all, and students can count on it, achievement rises (Marzano, 2006). So standardize procedures in your school; agree on a common grading scale; do not allow extra credit for different things (e.g., bringing in canned goods, attending the basketball game); and have the points on the assessment (both multiple-choice and constructed-response questions) be the same for all classes in the school. (This should be the same as the state test.) Different rules and procedures muddy the waters for students. Be consistent and clear.

areas. These strategies need to be intentionally taught to both the students and the parents, and the responsibility for following through with the strategies needs to fall on not only the entire staff, but also on the student and the parent. Specific planning needs to take place with clear targets and evidence of learning. Too often, teachers complain the most about students' lacking these types of skills. At the same time, teachers fail to determine exactly how they will be taught and who will teach them. By being deliberate in teaching these skills, we can ensure that students will take strategies with them that they can use in school and life beyond school.

Once their students have learned test-taking strategies, teachers can analyze their data and decide on future instruction knowing that the test itself is not skewing the results of learning. This will make it all the easier to determine what's really going on with the data. Only by taking the test-taking elephant out of the room will we be able to accurately analyze the data and go beyond it to make the instructional decisions that will have a significant impact on student achievement.

# CHAPTER 8

# Charting the Data for Improvement

*Without change there is no innovation, creativity or incentive for improvement. Those who initiate change will have a better opportunity to manage the change that is inevitable.*

—William Pollard

## Charting the Data: Necessity and Reward

Going beyond the data to change instruction means working on specific strategies to improve achievement. You look to the data to drive instructional decisions. When all is said and done, however, it's important to chart the data so that you will know if what you have done in response to the data has made a difference. This is especially important as we move students up through the educational system; we don't want to keep doing something if it isn't working. This is where the beginnings of vertical alignment—aligning what we do instructionally from grade to grade—comes into play. We need to be very purposeful about the strategies we use to teach students from year to year, subject to subject. And, we need to pass that information on so that there is no guessing. This chapter, then, will focus on how to chart the data to determine if the strategies implemented when going beyond the data to change instruction have in fact been successful and what to do when the strategies have not been successful. This chapter will also provide information on how to pass on the responsibility of compiling and analyzing the data to the students themselves. Research shows that when students track their own progress they take ownership of their learning which again leads to increased achievement and proficiency (Marzano, 2006).

# How to Chart Progress

Many times we compile data at one point in time, then wait a while and do it all over again. This is true for nationally standardized tests such as the Terra Nova or the Stanford, state assessments, and even short-cycle formative assessments. Data is provided for achievement at that particular point in time. Long-term data, such as year-by-year or grading-period-by-grading-period, aren't provided on a regular basis. We usually have the data in the form of electronic data or even cumulative folders (most of the time kept in the office), but again, it is all over the place. When charting improvements or progress, it's important to compile the data in one place. In other words, you need one chart or graph to show progress across time. Trends over time are really what lead to accurate and authentic analysis of data. To view trends over time, the data needs to span across time. That means a system needs to be in place for teachers in all grade levels and subject areas to both chart and pass on relevant data. This will take some effort and organization on the teacher's part, as well as the principal's part. Teachers will need to be dedicated to the process, and principals will need to ensure accountability for the process. That means a consistent system needs to be in place.

A simple chart will allow for easy compilation of the data long-term. When developing the chart, try to keep in mind what you're trying to track. If you're trying to track student progress on yearly state exams, then the chart will be fairly simple and could look something like the chart in Figure 8.1.

**Figure 8.1**  Data Chart for Yearly Progress

### State Test Results for the Class of 2014

| Subject | 2003-04 | 2004-05 | 2005-06 | 2006-07 | 2007-08 | 2008-09 | 2009-10 |
|---------|---------|---------|---------|---------|---------|---------|---------|
| Reading | 83% | 87% | 94% | 79% | 85% | 82% | 81% |
| Writing | 96% | 94% | 93% | 92% | 94% | 88% | 82% |
| Mathematics | 75% | 72% | 78% | 76% | 79% | 77% | 78% |
| Social Studies | 81% | 87% | 82% | 75% | 79% | 83% | 82% |
| Science | 65% | 67% | 62% | 69% | 67% | 66% | 76% |

If you are interested in tracking progress in a specific subject, standard, or skill, then the chart will be a little more involved. A more detailed chart is shown in Figure 8.2.

When creating a chart for progress, the most simple formula is to place the "what" in the horizontal rows and the "how" in the vertical columns. The "what" might be individual students if you're tracking a complete grade level. In this case, the "how" may be each student's overall score on a given assessment.

**■ Figure 8.2**    Data Chart for Yearly Progress by Subject and Standard

### State Results by Subject and Standard for the Class of 2014

| Subject | 2003-04 | 2004-05 | 2005-06 | 2006-07 | 2007-08 | 2008-09 | 2009-10 |
|---|---|---|---|---|---|---|---|
| **Reading** | **83%** | **87%** | **94%** | **79%** | **85%** | **82%** | **81%** |
| ◆ Phonemic Awareness | 82% | NA | NA | NA | NA | NA | NA |
| ◆ Acquisition of Vocabulary | 81% | 88% | 92% | 77% | 85% | 81% | 80% |
| ◆ Reading Comprehension | 85% | 86% | 96% | 79% | 84% | 79% | 78% |
| ◆ Informational Text | 84% | 86% | 92% | 78% | 86% | 80% | 83% |
| ◆ Literary Text | 83% | 85% | 94% | 79% | 85% | 84% | 81% |
| **Writing** | **96%** | **94%** | **93%** | **92%** | **94%** | **88%** | **82%** |
| ◆ Writing Conventions | 94% | 93% | 92% | 91% | 92% | 88% | 80% |
| ◆ Writing Applications | 95% | 95% | 93% | 94% | 94% | 78% | 81% |
| ◆ Writing Processes | 97% | 94% | 91% | 92% | 90% | 92% | 82% |
| ◆ Research | 96% | 94% | 93% | 92% | 94% | 91% | 81% |
| ◆ Oral Communication | 95% | 92% | 93% | 91% | 95% | 89% | 82% |
| **Mathematics** | **75%** | **72%** | **78%** | **76%** | **79%** | **77%** | **78%** |
| ◆ Number Sense | 74% | 71% | 78% | 76% | 79% | 76% | 77% |
| ◆ Measurement | 75% | 73% | 79% | 75% | 80% | 745 | 78% |
| ◆ Geometry | 74% | 72% | 80% | 77% | 81% | 78% | 79% |
| ◆ Algebra | 76% | 72% | 76% | 79% | 76% | 77% | 76% |
| ◆ Data Analysis | 73% | 71% | 77% | 70% | 77% | 76% | 80% |

If you're tracking multiple skills in a subject, you may want to create a chart for each student. In this case the "what" would be the specific skill (e.g., place value, addition facts, area and perimeter) and the "how" would be the descriptor of progress toward mastery (e.g., a check, plus or minus; a percentage score of an assessment; the words "developing", "proficient") For your convenience, a blank *Class Project Chart* and a blank *Individual Student Progress Chart* have been provided for you on pages 106 and 107 in the Blueprints section.

**Tip:** When deciding how to chart data over time, ask yourself this question, "What is it I really want to know?" Then, put the information together in such a way that you can answer that question.

## How to Display Improvement

In the same way that charting progress should be kept simple, displaying progress should also be kept simple. The difference between the points made here and in chapter 2 is that here we are referring to long-term data. This data is compiled over a series of time and is directed at the instruction that occurred as a result of the initial data. This is, if you will, the evidence that the analysis of data did indeed result in instructional changes that affected achievement.

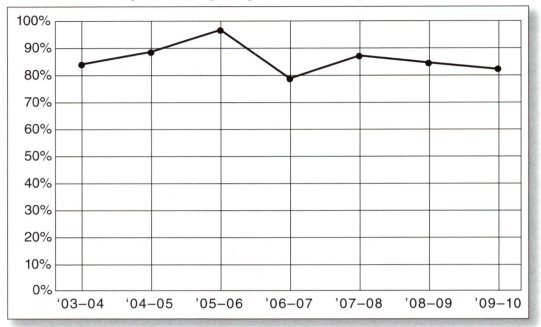

**Data Graph for Yearly Progress in Reading on State Tests**

The logical graph to choose to display this data is a line graph since a line graph is designed to show progress over time. In a line graph the "what" forms the x-axis, while the "how" forms the y-axis. The graph will vary depending on the type of data being compiled. For example, when displaying the data from Figure 8.1, the school years will make up the x-axis, and percentages will make up the y-axis. An example of this is shown in Figure 8.3.

If you want to display specific progress on specific standards as in Figure 8.2, then the x-axis would contain the school years, while the y-axis is made up of the descriptor of progress (e.g., percentages, evaluative words). Different color points would then make up the different standards. An example of this type of graph is shown in Figure 8.4.

Two different templates for line graphs such as these, *Class Progress Graph* and *Individual Student Progress Graph*, can be found on pages 108 and 109 in the Blueprints section.

## Student Involvement in Data

Allowing students to chart and make graphs of their own data can be a powerful motivational tool. Younger students will think it's fun to track their progress while older students will come to view their data as a natural part of the educational process. As with teachers, the process of data analysis should be kept simple. Students should be provided with a data notebook.

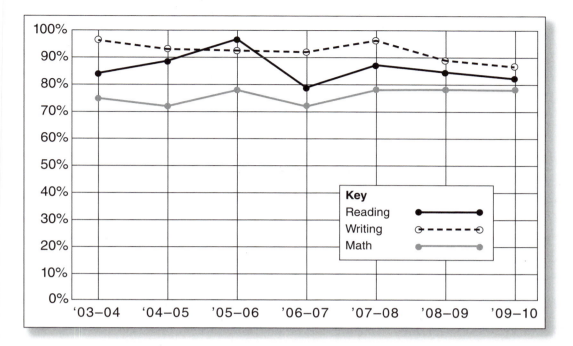

■ **Figure 8.4** Daily Graph for Yearly Progress by Subject

The notebook should contain all their important data. Depending on the circumstances the data may be compiled in one data notebook, or a notebook per subject area. The notebooks should be kept in one place that is accessible to the students at all times. It is probably not a good idea to let the students keep their data notebooks with them or take them home for the most part. An exception to this might be when students conduct a home, student-led conference with their parents, or perhaps when students are comparing data from different subject areas.

Keeping with the simple theme, the data should be simple and concise. Most of the charts and graphs provided in this book could be used by the students themselves. Other times, the charts and graphs may need to be adapted depending on the grade level of the student. Students could keep a virtual notebook—one in which the data is displayed, stored, and analyzed on a computer. Whichever process is used, it is important to note that students will need to be taught how to compile and display data. Many times this falls naturally into the academic content standards in math or science. Keeping their own data notebooks and analyzing their own data will also move students into higher level, critical thinking. This type of analysis can also lead to students themselves being able to suggest differentiated activities based on their interests or learning styles. If this process was implemented at the beginning of a student's journey through school, it would become an automatic part of the educational process.

An easy way to begin this process with students is to simply have them graph their percentage scores on subject-specific tests. These may be end-of-the-unit

**Tip:** After your students become proficient at compiling and analyzing their own data, consider having them lead their own conferences with their parents. Student-led conferences have been shown to have a powerful effect on learning and serves to keep the communication between the student, parent, and teacher open and real.

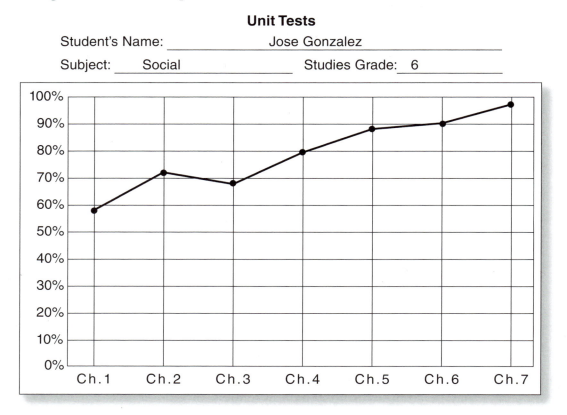

**Unit Tests**

Student's Name: _____ Jose Gonzalez _____

Subject: _____ Social _____ Studies Grade: _6_____

**Tip:** Consider displaying the data publically. Post by class, subject or grade level. Then, make a goal based on the graph and post that. For example, if the total score for one class in grade 6 is 75% in math for grading period 1, the goal might be "Our goal for grading period # 2 in math is 80%." Make it a competition between subjects, grade levels, or classes. Students love a competition!

tests, tests that come from textbooks, or even state-mandated tests. In this type of line graph, the x-axis would be the name of the test, while the y-axis would be the percentage score. An example of this type of graph is shown in Figure 8.5.

As students become more accomplished at graphing their data, they could move into more detailed data. This might include charting their progress on each content standard. To do this, the content standard would need to be provided for each question on an assessment. The students could then be given a piece of graph paper with the standard displayed in the column on the left hand side. Then, every time the student gets a correct answer on a test, they would color in the box next to the standard. In this way, the visual representation becomes a horizontal bar graph. This type of a graph could also be useful to the teacher as far as showing the frequency of assessing the standards. A teacher may discover that some standards are taught and assessed more than others, and this might be a factor in the results of the data. An example of a standard mastery graph is shown in Figure 8.6. In addition, a *Mastery Graph of the Standards* blank can be found on page 110 in the Blueprints section.

Having students compile and analyze their own data will lead to a greater understanding by the student of exactly what's been taught. Discussing the data and having the students write their own reflections of the data will also lead to increased understanding (and will even provide practice in writing!).

*I Have the Data…Now What?*

**■ Figure 8.6** Mastery Graph of the Standards

Student's Name: _____ Michael Parker _____

Subject: _____ Science _____ Grade _____ 10 _____

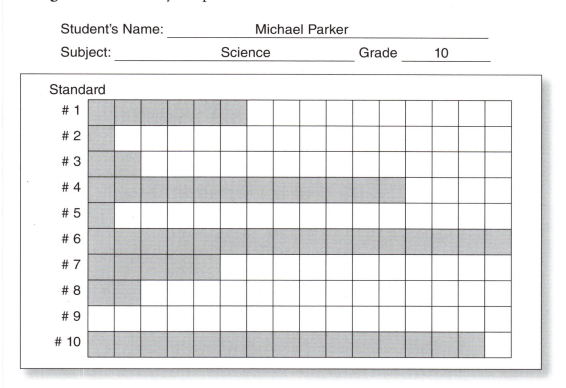

Many of the tools provided in this book for teachers when analyzing data can also be used by the students. It just means giving up some control.

## What to Do After Analyzing the Data

Data analysis should really be a cyclical process in which continued analysis is an intentional step. That means that if the data are not displaying the intended results, additional analysis and changes in instructional strategies may be necessary. It is about paying attention to details and becoming more specific in regard to instruction. This is no easy task, so analyzing the correct data in the correct way is essential. That means that data will continue to be revisited and that's why it's important to make the data relevant. Keeping clear records of pertinent data will lead to clear analysis, which in turn should lead to clear next steps. Those next steps may be participating in some type of professional development such as differentiated instruction strategies. Or, it may mean collaborating with the intervention specialist to provide different options for struggling students. It may mean co-teaching with a colleague so that tiered lessons can be implemented. Whatever the case, it is important to always remain active in your response to data.

**Tip:** When going beyond the data, ask the following questions:

♦ What do I want?

♦ How can I get what I want?

♦ How will I know I have gotten what I want? And the most important question:

♦ Is what I am doing best for kids?

## A Final Word on Charting the Data for Improvement

When charting the data for improvement, the most important thing to remember is that you're charting the data over a period of time. That means you may be keeping the data for more than one year. If this is the case, you'll need to keep the data so that it is easily accessible to whoever is viewing it, as well as easy to pass on to the next teacher. Charting the data for improvement may mean recording the data in a chart, or displaying it on a graph. It should be clear exactly what data is being monitored, and the data should always be displayed in a user- friendly way. Consider having the students themselves keep track of the data, which will teach some of the standards in math. In addition, research shows that when students have an active role in compiling and analyzing their own data, ownership for learning as well as achievement, increases. Whether the teacher charts the data for improvement, or the student charts the data, remember that analyzing the data is an active, ongoing process; one that will require constant adjustments in instruction and assessment. The goal is to determine if what we're doing instructionally is working—and if it isn't, adjusting what we're doing. In that respect, everyone wins.

# Epilogue:
# Where to Go From Here

*A journey of a thousand miles must begin with a single step.*
—Lao Tzu

When choosing to use data to influence instruction, there are several important things to keep in mind. The first thing is to keep both the data compilation and the display of the data as simple as possible. Keep all of the data in one place to be easily accessible. Also, try to limit the number of graphic representations of the data. Think about what you want to know, and what type of display will best represent what you want to know. Also, remember to analyze the data in a timely manner. If more than a week or two goes by, the data becomes cold and obsolete. Remember, "old data is cold data"!

When actually analyzing the data, carefully select the questions that you ask. You need to become an expert at looking for things that seem out of the ordinary. Try to approach the data analysis as an investigator on a crime scene. What looks out of place? Are there any trends you see? Also, look for the data that directly affects achievement. Then, go beyond that and ask yourself about the type, quantity, and quality of instruction. If you know you need to change something, but don't know what to do, educate yourself. Read books or attend a class. Talk with your peers and observe best-practice instructional strategies.

Deciding what to do once you have analyzed the data needs to be a systematic and intentional process. One such process is a six-step process:

**Step 1:** Displaying the Data in a User-Friendly Way

**Step 2:** Asking Questions About the Data

**Step 3:** Answering Questions Generated from the Data

**Step 4:** Forming Instructional Implications Implied by the Data

**Step 5:** Making Goals to Change the Results of the Data

**Step 6:** Knowing How to Assess the Goals

Perhaps the most important piece of this process is making goals that stem directly from the data and assessing those goals to see if progress has been made. Involved in these goals should be deliberate changes to instruction. One method of differentiation is called the Seven Steps for Instructional Change, a process consisting of intentional steps.

**Step 1:** Determine the area of instructional change.

**Step 2:** Determine ways to instruct the area that are different from the original mode of instruction.

**Step 3:** Determine the groups for instruction.

**Step 4:** Determine what instructional strategies will be used for each group, including details of what, how, where, and when.

**Step 5:** Determine how you will assess the learning.

**Step 6:** Determine what you will do in reaction to the information from the assessment.

**Step 7:** Determine how you will display the data to show if the instructional changes were effective.

There are several instructional changes that teachers can make to impact the data in step 4 of the Instructional Change Process. In reading, working on comprehension strategies will lead to achievement gains. Problem-solving skills are necessary in math if students are going to be successful. In writing, a lot of practice along with instruction on specific mechanics of writing needs to be provided on a regular basis. Providing students with the ability to read and analyze situations—especially information in graphic organizers—is a skill that will help to increase achievement in social studies, while teaching students the concept of cause and effect will impact science achievement. In addition, these are all skills that can influence all subject areas; in effect, these are essential skills for learning.

Two other areas for impacting achievement include teaching higher level, critical thinking skills, and test-taking skills. Teaching students how to analyze, synthesize, and evaluate will help them not only in the world of academics, but in the world beyond as well. Teaching test-taking as a genre will ensure that students are not tripped up by the vocabulary and structure of an assessment. Assessment for learning will then become the priority.

The last thing to do when using data to make instructional changes is to chart the data for improvement over time. It is also important not only to chart the improvement, but to pass the information on to the next teacher(s). Charting the data without sharing the data, or even having conversations about the data, is akin to doing nothing at all. Remember, the point of going beyond the data is to use the data to really make a difference in how teachers teach and students learn. One way this can be built into the school structure is through the RTI process, Response to Intervention. This process aligns itself nicely with analyzing data to change instruction since that is in essence what RTI does. The techniques and strategies in this book should fit in well with the RTI process, and in fact this process may indeed be the vehicle for the information to be stored and passed on.

As you embark on the journey to really go beyond the data to change instructional practices, consider several things. First of all, know that you're not alone. Most teachers have a large amount of data and a small amount of time, opportunity, and just basic know-how to analyze the data. Whenever possible, collaborate with other teachers. Consider forming a professional learning community, or pulling data analysis into the work of your already established PLC. Know that it's okay to start small and take baby steps; you don't have to do everything all at once. Also, don't be afraid to ask for help; if you need additional training in something, don't be afraid to read a book, attend a training, or simply ask a teacher or the curriculum specialist in your building for help. The most important thing to remember as you take this journey is to always be focused on the goal: what is the data telling you and what needs to be done? Then, simply (well, not simply!) find a way to do it. Remember, we want to get the most out of our students. That is, after all, why we do what we do.

# Blueprints
# for the Process

These reproducible worksheets should aid you in your journey to go beyond the data and make sure that the data is driving instructional decisions.

1. A Practical Data Analysis Timeline
2. Assessment Data Chart (blank)
3. Class Profile Graph (blank)
4. Item Analysis Graph (blank)
5. Questions Related to the Data
6. Classification of Questions and Answers from the Data Chart (blank)
7. Data Analysis Instructional Implications Chart # 1
8. Data Analysis Instructional Implications Chart # 2
9. Action Plan # 1
10. Action Plan # 2
11. Action Plan # 3
12. Goal Reaching Chart
13. A Plan for Instructional Change
14. Connections Chart

15. Problem Solving Strategy Record Keeper

16. Problem Solving Journal

17. Venn Diagram

18. Comparison Matrix

19. T Chart

20. Category Chart

21. Circle Category Chart

22. Cause and Effect Chart

23. What-So Chart

24. Analysis Chart

25. Synthesis Chart

26. Evaluation Chart

27. Standard and Test-Taking Alignment Chart

28. Skills in the Genre of Test-Taking Chart

29. Test Prep Contract

30. Student Posttest Reflections # 1

31. Student Posttest Reflections # 2 – Checklist

32. Student Posttest Reflections # 3 – Checklist for Younger Students

33. Class Progress Chart

34. Individual Student Progress Chart

35. Class Progress Graph

36. Individual Student Progress Graph

37. Mastery Graph of the Standards

## A Practical Data Analysis Timeline

| Type of Assessment | Compilation of Data | Analysis of Data |
|---|---|---|
| National Standardized Test | 3–4 Months | 2 Weeks |
| State Test | 3 Months | 2 Weeks |
| Short-Cycle Quarterly Assessment | 1 Week | 1 Week |
| Midterm/Final Exam | 1 Week | 1 Week |
| Subject Unit Test | 3 Days | 2 Days |
| Short Quiz | 1 Day | 1 Day |
| Formative Assessment: Observation, Quick Checks, etc. | Immediately | Immediately |
| Preassessment | 1 Day | Immediately following compilation to form flexible groups |

## Assessment Data Chart

**Directions:** In preparation for the data analysis, list your students' names in the column on the left. Then, write in the number of points earned for each question: 0, 1, 2, 3, or 4. Next, total the final %.

| Student's Name | 1 __ pts. | 2 __ pts. | 3 __ pts. | 4 __ pts. | 5 __ pts. | 6 __ pts. | 7 __ pts. | 8 __ pts. | 9 __ pts. | 10 __ pts. | 11 __ pts. | 12 __ pts. | 13 __ pts. | 14 __ pts. | 15 __ pts. | 16 __ pts. | 17 __ pts. | 18 __ pts. | 19 __ pts. | 20 __ pts. | % |
|---|---|---|---|---|---|---|---|---|---|---|---|---|---|---|---|---|---|---|---|---|---|
| | | | | | | | | | | | | | | | | | | | | | |
| | | | | | | | | | | | | | | | | | | | | | |
| | | | | | | | | | | | | | | | | | | | | | |
| | | | | | | | | | | | | | | | | | | | | | |
| | | | | | | | | | | | | | | | | | | | | | |
| | | | | | | | | | | | | | | | | | | | | | |
| | | | | | | | | | | | | | | | | | | | | | |
| | | | | | | | | | | | | | | | | | | | | | |
| | | | | | | | | | | | | | | | | | | | | | |
| | | | | | | | | | | | | | | | | | | | | | |
| | | | | | | | | | | | | | | | | | | | | | |
| | | | | | | | | | | | | | | | | | | | | | |
| Points Earned | | | | | | | | | | | | | | | | | | | | | |
| Possible Points | | | | | | | | | | | | | | | | | | | | | |
| % Mastery | | | | | | | | | | | | | | | | | | | | | |

## Class Profile Graph

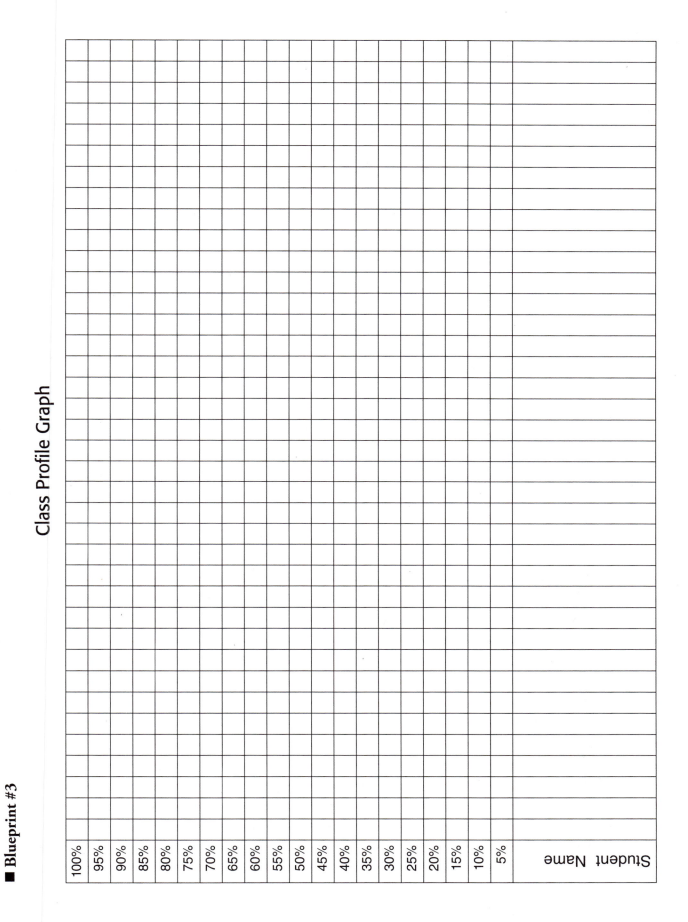

| | 100% | 95% | 90% | 85% | 80% | 75% | 70% | 65% | 60% | 55% | 50% | 45% | 40% | 35% | 30% | 25% | 20% | 15% | 10% | 5% |
|---|---|---|---|---|---|---|---|---|---|---|---|---|---|---|---|---|---|---|---|---|
| **Student Name** | | | | | | | | | | | | | | | | | | | | |

## Item Analysis Graph

| Question # | 1 | 2 | 3 | 4 | 5 | 6 | 7 | 8 | 9 | 10 | 11 | 12 | 13 | 14 | 15 | 16 | 17 | 18 | 19 | 20 | 21 | 22 | 23 | 24 | 25 |
|---|---|---|---|---|---|---|---|---|---|---|---|---|---|---|---|---|---|---|---|---|---|---|---|---|---|
| Standard | | | | | | | | | | | | | | | | | | | | | | | | | |
| 100% | | | | | | | | | | | | | | | | | | | | | | | | | |
| 90% | | | | | | | | | | | | | | | | | | | | | | | | | |
| 80% | | | | | | | | | | | | | | | | | | | | | | | | | |
| 70% | | | | | | | | | | | | | | | | | | | | | | | | | |
| 60% | | | | | | | | | | | | | | | | | | | | | | | | | |
| 50% | | | | | | | | | | | | | | | | | | | | | | | | | |
| 40% | | | | | | | | | | | | | | | | | | | | | | | | | |
| 30% | | | | | | | | | | | | | | | | | | | | | | | | | |
| 20% | | | | | | | | | | | | | | | | | | | | | | | | | |
| 10% | | | | | | | | | | | | | | | | | | | | | | | | | |
| 0% | | | | | | | | | | | | | | | | | | | | | | | | | |
| Actual points | | | | | | | | | | | | | | | | | | | | | | | | | |
| Possible points | | | | | | | | | | | | | | | | | | | | | | | | | |
| % mastered | | | | | | | | | | | | | | | | | | | | | | | | | |

## Questions Related to the Data

♦ Are there trends across a grade level on the most successful standards? On the least successful? On the format of the questions? On the level of the questions?

♦ Why did individual students perform as they did? What does that mean? What can you do about it?

♦ Were you satisfied with the data?

◇ Could you have predicted specific performances on specific questions? If yes, how did you use that information prior to the test administration?

♦ Looking at the data, what are the instructional implications? How will you implement them? What specifically will you do?

♦ How was the material taught for the questions that were the most successful?

◇ What materials were used that were particularly helpful?

◇ Did you provide differentiated instruction? If so, what did it look like?

♦ If your students need more practice with certain questions types/levels, what is your plan to provide them with this practice? Could you collaborate with other teachers who also have students with the same needs? What would this look like?

♦ Look at examples of classroom work for the work-connected assessment. Is the classroom work aligned with the assessment?

◇ For example, were the same graphic organizers used with the students? What about the vocabulary used? Did you instruct the students how to answer higher level questions? Constructed-response questions?

◇ Did the work your students do in the classroom everyday look like the type of work they would be asked to do on the work connected to the data?

♦ Did you take into account cultural or gender bias in both instruction and assessment? What do you think that would mean as far as the results of the data?

♦ Was there any connection between the time spent teaching certain standards and the student's performance on the questions assessing those standards? Could this indicate a change in the time spent on instruction of certain standards—either more time or less time?

♦ Were there any extenuating circumstances (e.g., weather-related days off, addition of extra-curricular mandates) that may have impacted the data? What does that mean?

♦ What are three goals to work on over the next grading period that will change the data next time? How will you know when the goals have been accomplished?

## Classification of Questions and Answers from the Data

| Topic | Question | Answer |
|-------|----------|--------|
|       |          |        |
|       |          |        |
|       |          |        |
|       |          |        |
|       |          |        |

*I Have the Data…Now What?*

# Data Analysis Instructional Implications Chart #1

| Key | |
|---|---|
| **MC** = Multiple Choice | **Lower Level** = Knowledge, Comprehension, Application |
| **CR** = Constructed Response | **Higher Level** = Analysis, Synthesis, Evaluation |
| | **Student Performance** = Poor, Fair, Excellent |

| Ques. | Standard | Ques. Type | Ques. Level | Student Performance | Instructional Implication |
|---|---|---|---|---|---|
| | | | | | |
| | | | | | |
| | | | | | |
| | | | | | |
| | | | | | |
| | | | | | |
| | | | | | |

# Data Analysis Instructional Implications Chart #2

| Key: | | |
|------|------|------|
| **MC**: Multiple Choice | **CR:** Constructed Response | **RG:** Response Grid |
| **HL:** Higher Level | **LL:** Lower Level | |

| Most Successful | | | | | | | Least Successful | | | | | | |
|---|---|---|---|---|---|---|---|---|---|---|---|---|---|
| Ques. | Standard | MC | CR | RG | HL | LL | Ques. | Standard | MC | CR | RG | HL | LL |
| | | | | | | | | | | | | | |
| | | | | | | | | | | | | | |
| | | | | | | | | | | | | | |
| | | | | | | | | | | | | | |
| | | | | | | | | | | | | | |
| | | | | | | | | | | | | | |
| | | | | | | | | | | | | | |
| | | | | | | | | | | | | | |

**Instructional Implications:**

# Action Plan # 1

| Instructional Implication | Goal | Strategy |
|---|---|---|
|  |  |  |
|  |  |  |
|  |  |  |

## Action Plan # 2

| Goal | |
|---|---|
| **Who?**<br>(Who is responsible for accomplishing the goal?) | |
| **What?**<br>(What exactly will be done to accomplish the goal?) | |
| **When?**<br>(When will the goal be accomplished? What is the time line for the goal?) | |
| **How?**<br>(How will the person responsible know the goal is accomplished? What is the evidence?) | |

■ **Blueprint #11**

## Action Plan #3

**Key:**

**Type of Question:** MC (Multiple Choice) CR (Constructed Response)
**Level of Question:** Lower Level or Higher Level
**Student Performance:** Poor, Fair, Excellent

| Ques. # | GLI | Type of Question | Level of Question | Student Performance | Instuctional Implication |
|---------|-----|------------------|-------------------|---------------------|--------------------------|
|         |     |                  |                   |                     |                          |
|         |     |                  |                   |                     | **Instructional Plan**   |

Blueprints for the Process

83

## Goal Reaching Chart

| Goal | Evidence<br>(What will you see?) | Evidence<br>(What will you see?) | Evidence<br>(What will you see?) |
|------|------|------|------|
|  |  |  |  |
|  |  |  |  |
|  |  |  |  |

*I Have the Data . . . Now What?*

## A Plan for Instructional Change

**Step #1:** Describe the area of instruction that needs to be changed below.

**Step #2:** Describe a different instructional strategy that can be used to teach the concept.

**Step #3:** List the names of the students who will be a part of each of the Instructional Change group(s).

**Step #4:** Describe in detail how the instruction will occur. Include what will happen, how it will happen, how long it will take, what materials are needed, etc.

**Step #5:** Describe how you will assess the learning.

**Step #6:** Describe what you will do for the students who continue to struggle with the concept.

Describe what you will do for the students who master the concept.

**Step #7:** Describe how you will display the data to show if the Instructional Change process was successful.

# Connections Chart

**Key:** T–S=text-self;  T–T=text-text;  T–W=text-world

| Title of Book | Page # | T–S | T–T | T–W | Response |
|---|---|---|---|---|---|
|  |  |  |  |  |  |
|  |  |  |  |  |  |
|  |  |  |  |  |  |
|  |  |  |  |  |  |
|  |  |  |  |  |  |
|  |  |  |  |  |  |
|  |  |  |  |  |  |

## Problem Solving Strategy Record Keeper

| Date Started | Problem | Strategy | Date Competed |
|---|---|---|---|
| | | | |
| | | | |
| | | | |
| | | | |
| | | | |
| | | | |
| | | | |
| | | | |
| | | | |
| | | | |
| | | | |
| | | | |
| | | | |
| | | | |
| | | | |
| | | | |

Developed by Beth Yockey; Grade 4 Math Teacher; Herbert Mills Elementary School; Reynoldsburg, Ohio

## Problem-Solving Journal

| | |
|---|---|
| What does the problem want you to find?? | |
| What important information did the problem give you? | |
| What strategy did you use to solve the problem? | |
| Does your answer make sense? Why or why not? | |

Developed by Beth Yockey; Grade 4 Math Teacher; Herbert Mills Elementary School; Reynoldsburg, Ohio

# Graphic Organizers for Comparison
## Venn Diagram

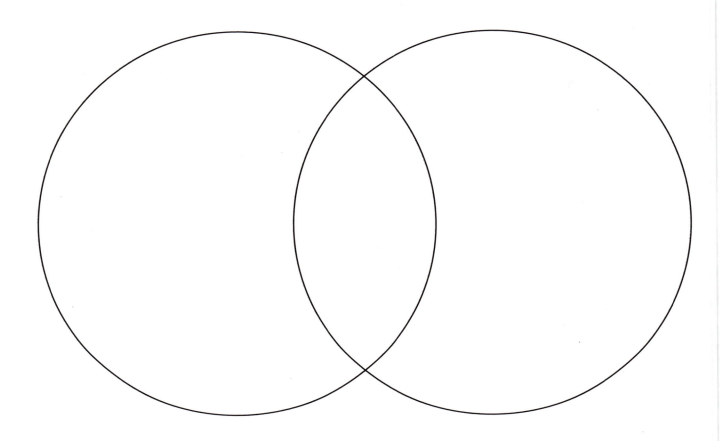

# Graphic Organizers for Comparison
## Comparison Matrix

| Characteristics | Items to be compared | | | |
|---|---|---|---|---|
| | #1 | #2 | #3 | |
| 1. | | | | Similarities |
| | | | | Differences |
| 2. | | | | Similarities |
| | | | | Differences |
| 3. | | | | Similarities |
| | | | | Differences |
| 4. | | | | Similarities |
| | | | | Differences |

# Graphic Organizers for Comparison
## T-Chart

| Item to Be Compared | |
|---|---|
| **Similarities** | **Differences** |
| | |

# Graphic Organizers for Comparison
## Category Chart

| Categories | | | | |
|---|---|---|---|---|
|  |  |  |  |  |
|  |  |  |  |  |

# Graphic Organizers for Comparison
## Circle Category Chart

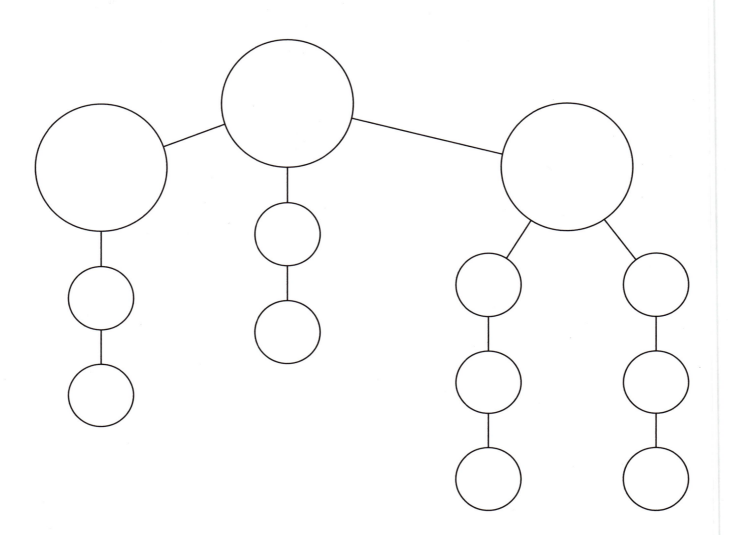

## Cause and Effect Chart

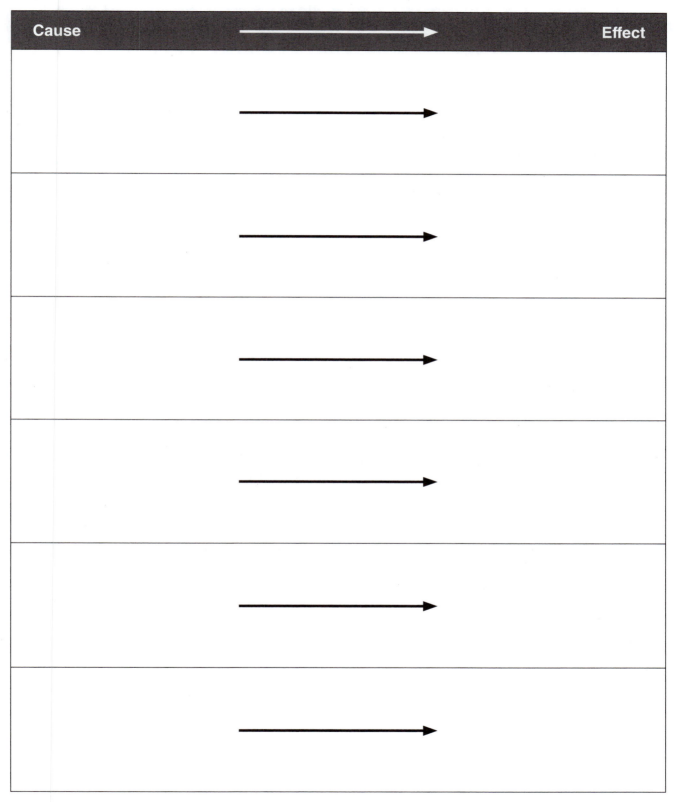

## What–So Chart

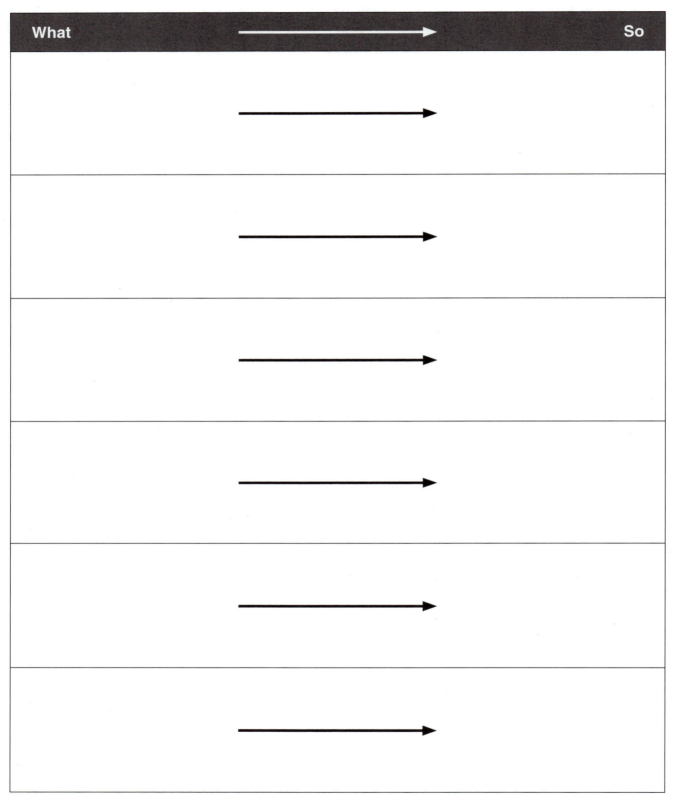

## Analysis Chart

1. Describe what was learned.



2. What do you have to know to really understand what was learned?



3. In what order would you need to learn the concepts in # 2 so you can understand what was learned in # 1?



4. Give an example of something that is similar to what you learned.

## Synthesis Chart

| |
|---|
| 1. Describe what was learned. |
| 2. What smaller things did you have to learn first? |
| 3. What is a different way to do what you learned? |
| 4. What would happen if _____ ? |

## Evaluation Chart

| |
|---|
| 1. Describe what was learned. |
| 2. What do you like the best about what was learned? |
| 3. Defend your opinion. Include several reasons. |
| 4. Argue the opposite opinion. |

## Standard and Test-Taking Alignment Chart

| Subject Area/Standard | Test-Taking Skills |
|---|---|
| | |

## Skills in the Genre of Test-Taking Chart

| Test/Test Item | Skills Needed to Answer the Question |
|---|---|
| | |

## Test Prep Contract

I, _____, promise that I will do the following prior to the test:

| Task | Date Completed | Initials |
|------|----------------|----------|
| _____ | _____ | _____ |
| _____ | _____ | _____ |
| _____ | _____ | _____ |
| _____ | _____ | _____ |
| _____ | _____ | _____ |
| _____ | _____ | _____ |
| _____ | _____ | _____ |
| _____ | _____ | _____ |
| _____ | _____ | _____ |

I understand that by doing or overseeing these tasks, I am increasing the chances for success on the test.

Signed _____

Date _____

Witness _____

## Student Posttest Reflections #1

Student's Name _____

Assessment _____ Date _____

1. The thing I liked best about the test was

2. The thing I liked least about the test was

3. I was/was not happy with the results of my test because

4. If I could do it over again, one thing I would change is

5. The type of questions I had the most difficulty with were

6. The reason I missed the items I did was because

7. My goal for next time is

# Student Posttest Reflections #2 Checklist

Student's Name _____

Assessment _____ Date _____

The questions I got correct on the test and the reasons for my success:

Question # _____          ☐ I knew the content          ☐ I got lucky and guessed.

Question # _____          ☐ I knew the content          ☐ I got lucky and guessed.

Question # _____          ☐ I knew the content          ☐ I got lucky and guessed.

Question # _____          ☐ I knew the content          ☐ I got lucky and guessed.

Question # _____          ☐ I knew the content          ☐ I got lucky and guessed.

Question # _____          ☐ I knew the content          ☐ I got lucky and guessed.

The questions I missed on the test and reasons I missed them:

Question # _____     ☐ I didn't know the content
                      ☐ I knew the content but was confused by the way the question
                         was asked.
                      ☐ I knew the content but just miscalculated; had a brain lapse, etc.

Question # _____     ☐ I didn't know the content.
                      ☐ I knew the content but was confused by the way the question
                         was asked.
                      ☐ I knew the content but just miscalculated; had a brain lapse, etc.

Question # _____     ☐ I didn't know the content.
                      ☐ I knew the content but was confused by the way the question
                         was asked.
                      ☐ I knew the content but just miscalculated; had a brain lapse, etc.

Question # _____     ☐ I didn't know the content.
                      ☐ I knew the content but was confused by the way the question
                         was asked.
                      ☐ I knew the content but just miscalculated; had a brain lapse, etc.

Question # _____     ☐ I didn't know the content .
                      ☐ I knew the content but was confused by the way the question
                         was asked.
                      ☐ I knew the content but just miscalculated; had a brain lapse, etc

# Student Posttest Reflections #3 Checklist for Younger Learners

Student's Name _____

Test _____

I liked taking the test.      😊      ☹

I knew everything on the test.      😊      ☹

I could have tried harder.      😊      ☹

I did my very best.      😊      ☹

I can't wait to take another test.      😊      ☹

## Class Progress Chart

| Subject | School Year ___ | School Year ___ | School Year ___ | School Year ___ | School Year ___ | School Year ___ | School Year ___ |
|---|---|---|---|---|---|---|---|
|  |  |  |  |  |  |  |  |
|  |  |  |  |  |  |  |  |
|  |  |  |  |  |  |  |  |
|  |  |  |  |  |  |  |  |
|  |  |  |  |  |  |  |  |
|  |  |  |  |  |  |  |  |
|  |  |  |  |  |  |  |  |
|  |  |  |  |  |  |  |  |
|  |  |  |  |  |  |  |  |
|  |  |  |  |  |  |  |  |
|  |  |  |  |  |  |  |  |
|  |  |  |  |  |  |  |  |
|  |  |  |  |  |  |  |  |

## Individual Student Progress Chart

| Subject | Standand | School Year ___ | School Year ___ | School Year ___ | School Year ___ | School Year ___ | School Year ___ |
|---------|----------|-----------------|-----------------|-----------------|-----------------|-----------------|-----------------|
|         |          |                 |                 |                 |                 |                 |                 |
|         |          |                 |                 |                 |                 |                 |                 |
|         |          |                 |                 |                 |                 |                 |                 |
|         |          |                 |                 |                 |                 |                 |                 |
|         |          |                 |                 |                 |                 |                 |                 |
|         |          |                 |                 |                 |                 |                 |                 |
|         |          |                 |                 |                 |                 |                 |                 |
|         |          |                 |                 |                 |                 |                 |                 |
|         |          |                 |                 |                 |                 |                 |                 |
|         |          |                 |                 |                 |                 |                 |                 |
|         |          |                 |                 |                 |                 |                 |                 |
|         |          |                 |                 |                 |                 |                 |                 |
|         |          |                 |                 |                 |                 |                 |                 |
|         |          |                 |                 |                 |                 |                 |                 |

## Class Progress Graph

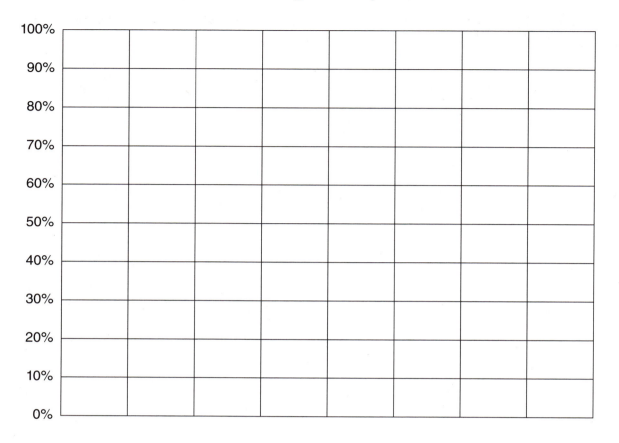

Name of Test

# Individual Student Progress Graph

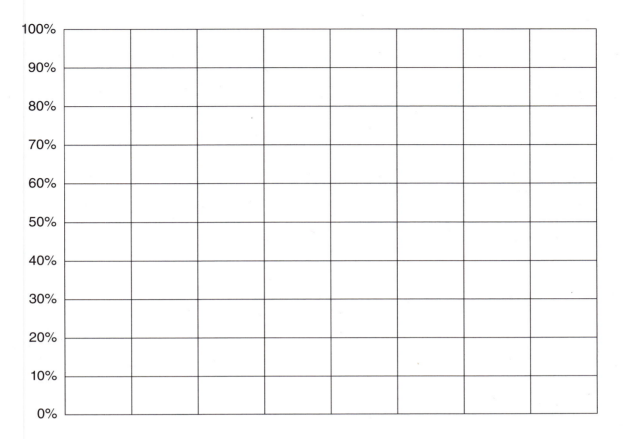

School Year

# Mastery Graph of the Standards

Student's Name _____

Assessment _____ Grade _____

**Standard**　　　　　　　　Key: ■ = mastered　　☐ = not mastered

| | | | | | | | | | | | | |
|---|---|---|---|---|---|---|---|---|---|---|---|---|
| | | | | | | | | | | | | |
| | | | | | | | | | | | | |
| | | | | | | | | | | | | |
| | | | | | | | | | | | | |
| | | | | | | | | | | | | |
| | | | | | | | | | | | | |
| | | | | | | | | | | | | |
| | | | | | | | | | | | | |
| | | | | | | | | | | | | |
| | | | | | | | | | | | | |
| | | | | | | | | | | | | |
| | | | | | | | | | | | | |
| | | | | | | | | | | | | |
| | | | | | | | | | | | | |
| | | | | | | | | | | | | |
| | | | | | | | | | | | | |
| | | | | | | | | | | | | |
| | | | | | | | | | | | | |

Developed by Kim Hartman; High School English Teacher; Watkins Memorial High School; Pataskala, Ohio

　　　　　　　　　　　　　　　　　　　*I Have the Data…Now What?*

# References

Anderson, L., Krathwohl, D., Airasian, P., & Cruikshank, K., Mayer, R., Pintrich, P., . . . Wittrock, M. (2000). *A taxonomy for learning, teaching and assessing: A revision of Bloom's taxonomy of educational objectives.* (Abridged ed). Boston: Allyn & Bacon.

Bangert-Downs, R. I., Kulik, C. C., Kulick, J. A. & Morgan, M. (1991). The instructional effects of feedback in test-like events. *Review of Educational Research, 61*(2), 213–238.

Barton, L. (1997). *Quick flip questions for critical thinking.* Dana Point, CA: Edupress.

Bernhardt, V. (2009). *Data, data everywhere.* Larchmont, NY: Eye on Education.

Bernhardt, V. (2007). *Translating data into information to improve teaching and learning.* Larchmont, NY: Eye on Education.

Lang, S., Stanley, T., & Moore, B. (2008). *Short-cycle assessment: Improving student achievement through formative assessment.* Larchmont, NY: Eye on Education.

Marzano, R. (2003). *What works in schools: Translating research into action.* Alexandria, VA: Association of Supervision and Curriculum Development.

Marzano, R. (2006). *Classroom assessment and grading that work.* Alexandria, VA: Association of Supervision and Curriculum Development.

Moore, B., & Stanley, T. (2010). *Critical thinking and formative assessment: Increasing the rigor in your classroom.* Larchmont, NY: Eye on Education.

Oberman, I., & Symonds, K. W. (2005). What matters most in closing the gap. *Leadership, 34*(3), pp. 8–11.

Schmoker, M. (2003) First things firsst: Demystifying data analysis. *Educational Leadership, 60*(5), 22–24

Stiggins, R., Arter, J., Chappuis, J., & Chappuis, S. (2006). *Classroom assessment for student learning.* Portland, OR: Educational Testing Service.

Tomlinson, C., & Allan, S. (2001). *How to differentiate instruction in mixed-ability classrooms.* Alexandria, VA: Association of Supervision and Curriculum Development.

Tomlinson, C., & McTighe, J.(2006). *Integrating differentiated instruction and understanding by design.* Alexandria, VA: Association of Supervision and Curriculum Development.

Wiggins, G., & Irua, L. (1997). *Educative assessment: Designing assessments to inform and improve student performance.* Hoboken, NJ: Jossey-Bass.

Wiggins, G., & McTighe, J. (1998). *Understanding by design.* Alexandria, VA: Association of Supervision and Curriculum Development.

Wiggins, G. (1998). A true test. Toward more authentic and equitable assessment. *Phi Delta Kappan, 70.*